Kim Campbell Thornton

Mastiffs

Everything About Purchase,
Care, Nutrition, Grooming,
Behavior, and Training

BARRON'S

CONTENTS

The Mastiff has a long history, first as a war dog, then as an estate guardian. These days, the breed is a kind companion, yet alert to danger. The Mastiff's size, good nature, and protective instincts have brought him increasing popularity.

"What the lion is to the cat, the Mastiff is to the dog, the noblest of the family; he stands alone and all others sink before him. His courage does not exceed his temper and generosity, and in attachment he equals the kindest of his race. His docility is perfect: the teasing of the smaller kinds will hardly provoke him to resent, and I have seen him down with his paw the terrier or the cur that has bit him without offering further injury. In a family he will permit the children to play with him, and suffer all their pranks without offense..."
—Sydenham Edwards, *Cynographia Brittanica*

The word mastiff has several possible origins, with lexicography suggesting that it comes from the Latin words *massivus,* meaning massive, or *mastinus,* meaning house dog. Another possibility is that it is derived from the Latin word *mansuetus,* meaning tame or gentle, a surprising origin given this breed's history as a fighter and warrior. Yet the Mastiff is indeed protective and gentle with his family, a result of centuries of service as a guardian of the home. While he can strike fear into the hearts of those who don't know him, the Mastiff is entirely worthy of the sobriquet "gentle giant," for he is good-natured and kind to all, save those who threaten his home and loved ones.

An Ancient Type

As is true of most breeds, there is little documented information about the origin of the Mastiff, and today's purebred Mastiff is of course not the same dog that was known 4,000 years ago. It is believed that the type originated in Tibet or northern India, where the Mastiff probably guarded flocks, a job for which his physique made it eminently suitable.

Giant dogs are distinguished by their massive size—a result of increased bone growth—heavy skulls, huge paws, and thick, loose, wrinkled skin, which on the face produces the characteristic scowl that enhances their reputation as dogs to be reckoned with. The smooth coat and loose skin play a protective role as well, precluding enemies from grasping and holding them.

The early Mastiff was known as a molosser or molossus. At that time, the science of genetics and the concept of breeding for type were unknown, and the molosser was no doubt quite different from the Mastiff we know today, which has been bred in its present form for less than two centuries. It was enough, then, that a dog be capable of fulfilling his purpose, whether that was guarding, hunting, or fighting. The Mastiff has been successfully used in all three occupations.

Travels Far and Wide

From their mountainous Asian origin, Mastiffs spread throughout the world, taken by traders and nomads to the Middle East, the Mediterranean, China, and Russia. The earliest depictions of Mastiff-type dogs are found on Egyptian monuments dating to about 3,000 B.C. Classical Greek art also depicts Mastiffs, as do Babylonian wall reliefs from the seventh century B.C. The first written mention of Mastiffs is from China, in a document dating to 1121 B.C. By 600 B.C., dogs known as Shejos—large, fierce, short-faced "hounds"—were found in China. In ancient times, the term hound was often used in reference to Mastiffs. In Greek mythology, three-headed Cerberus, who guards the entrance to Hades, is described as a Mastiff. Even Aristotle, in 350 B.C., mentions the progenitor of the Mastiff—the molosser—in a list of "most useful" breeds.

Dogs of War

Early in its history, the Mastiff had quite a reputation for ferocity. The civilizations of Assyria, Sumeria, Babylonia, Phoenicia—whose bold seafaring traders no doubt helped spread the Mastiff throughout the known world—Greece and Rome all made use of Mastiffs as war dogs. Outfitted with armor and wearing collars fitted with spikes, blades, or fiery torches, the dogs led the charge against the enemy.

Fighting Dogs

When they weren't being used on the battlefield, Mastiffs were kept in fighting trim by being pitted against other animals, either in the hunt or as a spectacle. Assurbanipal, a king of Assyria during the seventh century B.C., kept many Mastiff-type dogs to hunt lions and wild horses. Clay tablets from the period show the dogs being restrained by men holding leashes. But not everyone was aware of the Mastiff's courage and boldness. Cyrus the Great of Persia was sent a Mastiff by the king of Albania. When Cyrus pitted the Mastiff against one of his own dogs, and then a bull, he was disappointed in its performance and had it killed. The Albanian king heard of this and sent Cyrus a Mastiff bitch with a message: "The Mastiff is no ordinary cur," he wrote. "You must present it with a worthy opponent such as a lion or elephant." This Cyrus did, and Herodotus reports that the Mastiff went after the elephant with fury, driving it to the ground. While this story probably has only a tiny grain of truth, it does link the Mastiff with Albania, whose people were known as the Alani. Mastiffs have been called Alano, Alan, and Alaunt, and it is certainly possible that they were well known and appreciated in that tough, mountainous country, which then was populated by warlike Illyrians and Thracians.

Besides being courageous, Mastiffs were loyal, even unto death. Of a later Persian king and his Mastiff, Aelian wrote, "When Darius, the last of the Persian kings, was killed by Bessus in his battle with Alexander, and lay dead, all the men left the corpse behind but the dog alone he had bred remained faithful."

The Mastiff's ancestors originated in the mountains of Asia. From there, they spread throughout the ancient world and evolved into the breed we know today.

Aelian continues his paean to the Mastiff, writing: "The dog belonging to King Lysimachus chose to die by the same fate as his master, although he could, had he so wished, have saved himself. Again, when there was civil war in Rome, a Roman citizen called Calvus was killed. Many of his enemies strove in rivalry to accomplish the glorious deed of cutting off his head, but none could do so until they had killed the dog who stood by his side."

The Celtic tribes of Europe and Britain also had ferocious Mastiffs, which were written of admiringly by Julius Caesar, who noted their power and courage. A historian of the time reported that after the Romans defeated one such tribe in battle, they had to fight another battle against the dogs guarding the tribe's encampment. The Romans took some of these dogs back to Rome, where they were matched against human gladiators, bulls, bears, lions, and tigers in the Colosseum.

From War Dog to Guardian

When William the Conqueror invaded Britain and Norman French became the language of choice, the French word *dogue,* which referred to Mastiffs, became the commonly used term for all dogs in England, because Mastiffs were so common there. Mastiffs prowled estates at night, keeping wolves and human predators such as poachers and other criminals at bay. These dogs were so fierce that many people believed they were the result of crosses with bears and wolves. During the day, they were tied, giving rise to the name bandog or tiedog. To keep crime down, the law required a ratio of one Mastiff for each two "villeins," or villagers. But to prevent the peasants' dogs from taking any game rightfully belonging to the lord, dogs of a certain size were mutilated by having their first three toes chopped off—a practice called expediating—rendering them unable to run down hares or deer.

The Mastiff's reputation for bravery as well as hunting ability continued throughout the Middle Ages. In the late thirteenth century, when Marco Polo returned from his sojourn in China, he described Kublai Khan's pack of 5,000 Mastiffs, writing: "Truly it is a glorious sight to see the working of the dogs and the huntsmen on such an occasion . . . you will see these big hounds come tearing up, one pack after a bear, another pack after a stag, or some other beast. . . ." In his fourteenth-century story *Knight's Tale,* Chaucer describes packs of Mastiffs, also known as Alaunts, being used to hunt lion and deer. Chaucer describes the dogs as white and as large as steers, the latter a claim that strains credulity.

As late as the fifteenth and sixteenth centuries, Mastiffs were still being used in wars. At the Battle of Agincourt in 1415, the Mastiff bitch of Sir Piers Legh of Lyme Hall guarded her wounded master for hours until he could

be rescued from the field. Sir Piers later died of his wounds in Paris, but the faithful Mastiff was sent back to Lyme Hall where she became the foundation for the famous Lyme Hall strain, which continued until the early twentieth century and on which the modern English Mastiff is based. A stained glass window at Lyme Hall depicts Legh and his Mastiff.

Fit for a King

Mastiffs also made fine gifts from one king to another. Henry VIII sent a battalion of 400 Mastiffs to the Holy Roman Emperor Charles V, who was also Charles I of Spain. Perhaps it was one of those dogs that wore the sixteenth century canine armor now on display in Madrid's Museum of Artillery.

The Mastiff was quite a well-known type of dog by the sixteenth century. Johannes Caius, the Elizabethan-era author who wrote *Of Englishe Dogges,* described the Mastiff, which he called a bandog, thusly: "vaste, stubborn, ougly . . . of a burthenous body . . . terrible and frightful to behold." Another book of the time, *Foure Bookes of Husbandrie,* published in 1586, offered the following advice about Mastiffs: "In choosing a Mastie that keepeth the house, you must provide such a one as hath a large, mightie bodie and a great shrill voice, that both with its barking may discover and with its sight dismay the thief."

Brutal "Entertainment"

While Mastiff-type dogs had always been great favorites in fighting pits, it was during the Elizabethan era that their role truly began to evolve from fighting in wars to fighting in so-called "entertainments." Until 1835, with a brief respite in the mid-seventeenth century when

Parliament banned the practice, Mastiffs were used in bearbaiting, bullbaiting, and dogfights, and even against men armed with pikestaffs and clubs, according to Caius. Such entertainments were attended by people of all classes, from the nobility and clergy to the working poor, with wagers being placed on which animal might win. Queen Elizabeth I even went so far as to restrict plays and other entertainments on Thursday nights so that no one—herself included—would miss the bullbaiting. It was also during this period, however, that Mastiffs and other dogs began to wear the trappings that proclaimed them the valued possessions of the nobility. In her book *The Lost History of the Canine Race*, anthropologist Mary Thurston tells us that prized Mastiffs wore solid bands of bronze, silver, or gold, emblazoned with griffins, lions, or other symbols of power.

The Modern Mastiff

The year 1835 was a pivotal one for the Mastiff. It was then that T. H. V. Lukey decided to restore the breed to what he believed to be its original form, breeding a brindle bitch purchased from the Duke of Devonshire to a dog purchased from Lord Waldegrave. Other men who influenced the development of the Mastiff to its current form were Captain J. E. Garnier, a breeder, and Bill George, a well-known dealer in dogs. It is from the dogs produced by the Duke of Devonshire's bitch and the Lyme Hall strain of Mastiffs that today's Mastiff is descended.

The other occurrence of 1835 that affected the Mastiff—both positively and negatively—was that the brutal "sports" of dogfighting and bull- and bearbaiting were outlawed. This was positive, of course, as a step forward in the humane treatment of animals, but even so, the law was flouted for at least another 20 years. Eventually, however, interest in the breed declined as the practice of pitfighting waned, leading to a reduction in the dogs' numbers. Industrialization reduced the incidence of poachers on great estates, for a further decline in the breed's popularity. However, the breed was being exhibited in 1860, with Mr. Hanbury's Empress taking first place at a dog show in Birmingham. A show in 1871 had an entry of 63 Mastiffs. By 1883 there was enough interest in the breed for the formation of the Old English Mastiff Club, which is now one of the oldest breed clubs in continuous existence. A Mastiff exhibit sponsored by the Old English Mastiff Club in 1890 drew 51 entries. Less than two decades later, the breed was in serious trouble. The food shortages that occurred in Britain in World Wars I and II contributed to a precipitous decline in the Mastiff's numbers, and in 1945, Britain was left with almost no Mastiffs of breedable age. Without the contributions of a pair of Canadian Mastiff pups, the breed might have died out entirely in its homeland.

The Mastiff in America

It's probable that the Mastiff made its way to this country during colonial times, but it was not until the late nineteenth century that the breed made much of an impact. The first American Mastiff Club was formed in 1879, and the years from 1885 to 1899 have been described as its golden age. The breed was recognized by the American Kennel Club (AKC) in 1885, with a dog named Bayard being the first Mastiff registered. The American Mastiff Club disbanded, however, and it was not until 1920 that the Mastiff Club of America was organized. Then it, too, fell by the wayside. The present Mastiff Club of America (MCOA) was established in 1929.

The Mastiff Imprint

Breeds influenced by or related to the Mastiff are many. They include the Bullmastiff, Dogo Argentino, Dogue de Bordeaux, Fila Brasileiro, Tibetan Mastiff, the Pug—a Mastiff in miniature—Saint Bernard, Great Dane, Neapolitan Mastiff, Spanish Mastiff, Pyrenean Mastiff, Bulldog, American Pit Bull Terrier, Rottweiler, Staffordshire Bull Terrier, American Staffordshire Terrier, Boxer, Bull Terrier, Boston Terrier, French Bulldog, Bernese Mountain Dog, Greater Swiss Mountain Dog, Entelbucher, Newfoundland, Tosa Inu, Leonberger, and Doberman Pinscher.

The Mastiff in Art

Because of its importance in the daily life of noble and royal families, the Mastiff is well represented in the art of the past three centuries. Two of the best-known portrayals of Mastiffs are the paintings *Las Meninas* by Spanish artist Diego Velasquez, and *The Children of Charles I* by English court painter Anthony Van Dyck. In the work *The Dog Market* (1677), Dutch artist Abraham Hondius depicts a variety of breeds, with a fawn Mastiff and a white and tan Mastiff-looking dog being most prominent. One eighteenth-century historian described the piece, which had just been sold at auction, as Hondius' masterpiece. Hondius also painted *Bear Baiting* (1650), a graphic depiction of four Mastiffs attacking a bear. A portrait of Lord Lempster (1685), attributed to Sir Peter Lely, is an example of the by then well-established tradition of the sitter with his or her dog, in this case a fawn Mastiff. In Antonio Moro's *Cardinal de Granville's Dwarf,* the size and power of the Mastiff are made all the more apparent by comparison to the small man with whom it is pictured. Not surprisingly, the Mastiff is frequently portrayed in a fight, as seen in such works as *Dogs Fighting* (1809) by Charles Towne.

Evolution in Art

Through art, we can also see the evolution of the Mastiff type. *Lion,* a portrait of a Mastiff painted by James Lambert, Sr. in 1778, shows a dog that is very different from the one painted by Philip Reinagle only 15 years later. In *Mastiff and a Landseer* (1792), attributed to George Charles Morland, we see a dog whose appearance is somewhere between that of Lambert's *Lion* and Reinagle's *Mastiff.*

The Victorian era was the heyday of dog portraiture, and Mastiffs are well represented

In his portrait of the English royal children, Sir Anthony Van Dyck includes the Mastiff, a symbol of the king's power.

in the art of this period, primarily in domestic scenes rather than the violence of earlier eras. In fact, a work by William Henry Trood is entitled just that: *A Domestic Scene* (1888). In it lies a Mastiff on an Oriental rug, surrounded by smaller dogs, one cradled between his paws, one climbing on him, another by his side, while a Bloodhound and several other dogs look on. *The Mastiff Lara* (1882) by H. Hardy Simpson depicts the dog in profile, a pose that soon became standard for portraying show dogs. Other works showing the Mastiff in peaceful situations include *Mastiff with a Terrier* (1871) by R. S. Moseley and *In Times of Peace* (1877) by Edwin Frederick Holt. An exception to the domesticity of these works is Richard Ansdell's *The Poacher* (1865), an earlier painting showing a Mastiff pinning a poacher to the ground.

Baskervilles Inspiration?

Mastiffs are not commonly found in literature. American novelist James Fenimore Cooper mentioned them in his stories, and England's poet laureate, Alfred, Lord Tennyson, depicted the Mastiff's kind nature in his poem *Queen Mary*, a stanza of which reads: "A Mastiff dog/May love a puppy cur for no more reason/Than the twain have been tied up together." A Mastiff called Derby the Devil Dog is believed to have been the inspiration for Sir Arthur Conan Doyle's tale of terror, *The Hound of the Baskervilles.*

THE FAMILY MASTIFF

Mastiffs have special needs that call for just the right family and home environment. Their great size requires a living area with plenty of space for them to move around. Drawbacks include a propensity to drool, potential orthopedic problems, and a shorter than average lifespan.

Owning a Mastiff

There is a Latin word, *gravitas*, meaning dignity or sobriety of bearing, qualities that are integral to this breed. A sober mien—albeit with an underlying sense of humor—calmness, and gentleness are the hallmarks of the Mastiff, a great beast with seriousness of purpose that gives the impression of having everything under control. People who live with Mastiffs credit them with great wisdom and depth of feeling.

While it is certainly a jumbo-size dog, you don't need to live on an estate to make a Mastiff part of your household. With an owner committed to giving him daily exercise, a Mastiff can adapt quite well to life in an apartment or condominium (ideally one without stairs), but a house with a yard is an ideal situation for this giant breed, which stands a minimum of 27 to 30 inches (68–76 cm) at the shoulder and weighs 120 to 230 pounds (54–104 kg) and sometimes more. The huge size and protective nature make the Mastiff a fine loyal dog for the family that has space for him and children old enough to interact safely and properly with him. While a proper Mastiff would never knowingly hurt a child, a single thwack of his tail could send a toddler sprawling.

The Mastiff's short coat is easy to care for, requiring only a simple brushing once a week, but like all dogs, he does shed. He also snores, sometimes quite loudly, and is prone to flatulence. Drool is another aspect of living with a Mastiff that you should consider. You'll need a good supply of hand towels or paper towels to dry your Mastiff's mouth after drinking or when the weather is hot. One young Mastiff learned quickly to grab his drool towel, run to the back door, and wait with it when he heard the garage door open, the signal that his master—wearing a nice suit—was home from work.

Toward his family, the Mastiff has a gentle, affectionate personality and a strong desire to be with people. The typical Mastiff is content to lie by a chair, leaning up against you or warming your feet, and following you from room to room as you go about your business. Some Mastiffs seem unaware of their immense size and enjoy snuggling on the sofa with their people, fitting into as much lap as possible. There's nothing more wonderful than coming home from a hard day at work, changing

Mastiffs are more sedate than some other breeds, but like every dog, they need training to learn how to walk politely with all family members.

From the Mastiff's long heritage as a guardian, from flocks to estates, the Mastiff has a protective, territorial nature. He barks to announce people at the door or passing by the home. Strangers who approach the Mastiff's family, especially children, or his home territory, which can be the house, the yard or the car, will be met with deep ferocious woofs. Should they be foolish enough to continue without your permission or escort, it is likely that the Mastiff will use his size and imposing presence either to prevent them from going farther or from leaving the premises until you arrive to release them. The Mastiff is not an attack dog, but he will take whatever steps he believes necessary to protect his family and home. Invited guests, however, are the Mastiff's delight. He enjoys watching the activity at parties and occasionally contributing his input to conversations.

Possible Drawbacks

As a potential Mastiff owner, one thing you should consider is whether the dog's size will affect your life in ways you might not have thought about. For instance, is your car large enough to hold a full-grown Mastiff? The puppy you take home may fit fine in your compact car, but it will be a different story six months later.

Veterinary bills can match the dog's giant size. Medications are often prescribed based on a dog's weight. A dog that weighs 200 pounds (91 kg) will require much more of a drug than

clothes, and settling down with this great, calm beast whose very presence is reassuring.

Like every dog, a Mastiff should be socialized from an early age to interact politely with other animals outside the family home, such as dogs in parks or training classes or cats on the street. The more types of dogs—and people—you familiarize your Mastiff with, the better, since this is a breed whose sheer size can make it unwittingly dangerous if he hasn't learned the rules of proper social intercourse. Nevertheless, the Mastiff is famed for its soft mouth and gentleness with creatures smaller than itself. One couple, who noticed their Mastiff carrying something around in the yard, pried his mouth open only to discover a very soggy baby squirrel, frightened but otherwise none the worse for wear.

one that weighs only 20 pounds (9 kg); for instance, monthly heartworm preventive for a single Mastiff can cost $125 to $150 a year.

And, of course, most people wonder if a Mastiff will eat them out of house and home. Depending on his size, the full-grown Mastiff eats only four to eight cups of food a day, which isn't that much for a dog of this size. On the other hand, if your Mastiff is a chewer, he may indeed eat you out of house and home—literally. A Mastiff can chew up a piece of furniture or a linoleum floor without even thinking about it. You'll need to watch your little Samson closely in puppyhood and keep a good supply of hard rubber toys and other sturdy chews on hand to substitute for things he shouldn't chew, such as your favorite recliner.

Exercise

The Mastiff's activity level is moderate, making it a nice choice for people who prefer short walks or gentle hikes to long runs or bicycle rides. Expect your Samson to stay by your side rather than bounding off to explore. He needs and enjoys daily exercise, but he won't run you off your feet the way a retriever or Border Collie might. But don't think that rules out competitive dog sports. Besides Conformation and Obedience, the Mastiff excels at the canine equivalent of power-lifting—weight pulling. Mastiffs can compete in Obedience and Rally Obedience. Some have even been known to enjoy the canine sports of Agility and Flyball. Other Mastiffs enjoy playing in the water and will run through sprinklers, stand in the rain, beg to be sprayed with the hose, or splash around in lakes or pools. Finally, the Mastiff's gentle, biddable nature makes it an ideal therapy dog.

Mastiffs and Other Pets

If raised with other dogs and cats, Mastiffs are friendly and get along well with them. Your cat may object to being drooled on by the Mastiff, but that is likely to be the only problem you encounter with the two. Of course, you'll need to be careful about the interactions you permit if your other dog is a small, fragile breed such as an Italian Greyhound or Chihuahua. Without meaning any harm, your Mastiff could injure such a small dog by playing too roughly. Like most dogs, Mastiffs recognize their own kind and especially enjoy being around others of their breed.

Conservative Dog

In many ways, the Mastiff is a special-needs breed, not only because of its great size but also because of the strong attachments he forms to his people and surroundings. The Mastiff is a conservative dog who detests change of any sort. He gives his whole heart to his family and often acts as peacemaker, stepping in to prevent children from being spanked and fretting when family members argue. He will grieve the loss of his family, so if you decide to get a Mastiff—or any dog, for that matter—he should be for keeps. This breed's loyalty and devotion should be rewarded by a lifelong home. If you are thinking of purchasing a Mastiff, or have recently acquired one, this book will help you understand and live in harmony with your new companion. In the following pages, you'll find tips on training, grooming, nutrition and health care, along with color photos and descriptive illustrations. As well as being a guide to Mastiff ownership, this book will be a keepsake that you will treasure and turn to again and again over the years with your special dog.

Producing a healthy litter of Mastiff puppies requires health testing of the parents to ensure that they are free of genetic diseases that could be passed on to the next generation, as well as good nutrition and clean living conditions. Visiting a breeder's home and seeing puppies and their relatives in the flesh is the best way to ensure that your new family member has had a good start in life.

Choosing a Breeder

Because giant breeds are prone to a number of health problems and tend to have shorter-than-average lifespans, finding the right source for your new puppy is the most important part of the buying process. A good breeder is hard to find and is a treasure to be prized once located. What makes a good breeder? Look for someone who is knowledgeable and experienced, who loves Mastiffs and wants only the best for them, and who gives his or her dogs excellent care and training.

How can you identify this jewel? A good breeder has been involved in Mastiffs—owning, showing, and breeding them—for at least five years. Length of time indicates commitment. Of course, someone who has been in the breed for less time can still be a good breeder, but ideally that person is being guided by someone more experienced.

Why is it important that breeders show their Mastiffs? After all, you're looking for a companion, not necessarily a show dog. But a dog show is more than just a beauty contest. It's an opportunity for breeders to display the results of their breeding programs for evaluation by other breeders and judges. Exhibiting a dog requires a commitment to a sound breeding plan as well as to an individual dog's good health, grooming, and character. Breeders who show their Mastiffs generally feed high-quality food, ensure that their dogs have all the necessary vaccinations to protect them from disease, and socialize their pups by exposing them at an early age to all kinds of people, places, sounds, noises, and smells.

In addition, they are concerned about producing healthy, high-quality dogs. A good breeder tests animals for genetic disorders before breeding so diseases won't be passed on to pups. Some of the hereditary and developmental conditions that affect Mastiffs are hip dysplasia, osteochondritis dissecans, and progressive retinal atrophy. Walk away from breeders who say genetic testing is worthless or that their lines don't have any problems.

If you can't travel to a breeder's home yourself, ask a friend or relative in the area to investigate for you or contact the references provided by the breeder to see if they're pleased with their puppies.

Whether a pup's parents have earned championships or have been tested for genetic problems before being bred may not seem important if you are acquiring a Mastiff solely as a companion, but financially savvy pet owners know that a dog's health and character rely in part on how good a start that dog had in life.

To find a good breeder, start by contacting the national breed club (listed on page 92) for a list of recommendations. Even if the breeder you contact doesn't have puppies available, he or she may be able to refer you to someone else.

Attending dog shows is another good way to find breeders. You will meet local breeders there, as well as some from out of town. Most breeders are happy to talk about their dogs and share their experiences with you. Talk to several breeders so you can get a good, all-around picture of the Mastiff. This is not a breed you should get without having seen at

least one adult in the flesh. Then you can begin your search for a puppy in earnest.

Evaluating the Breeder's Environment

- Whenever possible, visit the breeder's home and view the dogs' facilities. They should be clean and well kept. Avoid breeders who aren't willing to permit home visits. You should be able to determine for yourself whether your pup has been raised in an environment that is sanitary and conducive to home life. If you're buying a puppy long-distance, see if a friend or relative can visit the breeder, or ask for references from other puppy buyers.
- Meet the parents of the puppies, or at least the mother. You can often judge a pup's potential by his parents' appearance and temperaments. A shy or nervous mother is likely to pass on those traits to her pups. If one parent isn't available, ask to see photos or videos. Ask the

age of the parents. Mastiffs that are less than two years old are not yet fully mature, so avoid buying puppies produced by them.

• Don't feel obligated to buy from the first litter you see. The more Mastiffs you meet, the better picture you will get of the breed and the more knowledgeable you will become about choosing just the right Mastiff for you.

Price

Mastiffs are expensive. You can expect to pay $1,500 to $2,500 or more for a good-quality puppy.

Purchase Contract

When you are ready to buy, don't be surprised if you are asked to sign a purchase contract. This is a sign that a breeder takes seriously his or her responsibilities to both puppy and buyer. The contract should cover the rights of buyer and seller, any health guarantees, buy-back or return policies, spay/neuter requirements, and delivery of registration papers. A truly committed and responsible breeder will include a clause in the contract requiring that the Mastiff be returned to the breeder if for any reason the new owner cannot keep him.

Beware the breeder who paints a glowing picture of life with a Mastiff. No breed is perfect for everyone, and giant breeds have special considerations that should be taken into account before purchase.

The Right Puppy

Once you've found a good breeder, the fun part begins: looking at and choosing from among the puppies. Like all puppies, baby Mastiffs are cute and cuddly with big dark eyes

that seem to say, "Take me home." Even so, at eight weeks of age they already show the promise of their tremendous future size, with large paws and heavy heads.

They all seem irresistible, but your choice will be made easier once you decide whether you want a male or female, which color appeals to you, and whether you want to show the pup or simply have it as a companion. Some breeders will make the decision for you, taking into account your preferences and lifestyle and their observations of the litter. Take the recommendation seriously; breeders have been watching their pups on a daily basis for at least eight weeks and are well aware of their personalities by this point.

When choosing a puppy, think about what you expect from your Mastiff. If you want a

Ten Questions to Ask Breeders

1 Do you belong to national and local Mastiff clubs?
2 How long have you been breeding Mastiffs?
3 Do you have any other breeds?
4 How many litters have you bred?
5 What are the most serious problems Mastiffs have?
6 What is it like to train a Mastiff?
7 What temperament problems might a Mastiff have?
8 What behavior problems can I expect?
9 What type of contract, conditions, or guarantees are involved in the sale of the puppy?
10 Can you give me references from other puppy buyers?

companion, look for the puppy who enjoys being petted or held. Mastiff puppies range from cautious to inquisitive to full-tilt boogie in their approaches to people. They may or may not run right up to you, but they should never be cowering in a corner. The fearful or shy puppy is difficult to raise and may never out-grow these traits.

If your goal is to show your dog, you'll want a pup with physical characteristics indicating that he is likely to mature into a good or excellent specimen of the breed. These include a good square head, dense bone, and a coat that is not too heavy or long. Always share your expectations with the breeder so he or she can help you make the right decision.

Male or Female?

Generally, there is no reason to prefer one sex over the other, except size. Males are usually at least 20 pounds (9 kg) heavier and 2 inches (5 cm) taller than females. As far as personality

Ten Questions Breeders Will Ask You

1 Why do you want a Mastiff?
2 What do you know about the breed?
3 Have you owned a dog before and how long did he live?
4 Do you own your own home?
5 Do you have a fenced yard?
6 What kind of shelter do you have for the dog when he's outside?
7 How much time do you plan to spend with your Mastiff?
8 How will a Mastiff fit into your lifestyle?
9 Do you have children and how old are they?
10 Will you spay or neuter a pet-quality dog?

goes, Mastiffs are just as individual as anyone else. Bitches tend to be quieter, kinder, and more docile than dogs, who often have funny,

sweet, but busy personalities. Bitches that have not been spayed are sometimes moody. Bitches also tend to show "watchdog" qualities earlier than dogs and may be quicker to alert to strange noises or people. Both sexes are equally fond of children and will take it upon themselves to act as guardian and surrogate parent.

Whatever sex you choose, you must decide whether and when to spay or neuter your Mastiff. Dogs that will be shown in Conformation may not be altered until their show careers have ended. Pet Mastiffs should be spayed or neutered. Spay/neuter surgery has some health benefits, including a lower risk of mammary cancer in females and elimination

Before You Breed Your Mastiff

Mastiffs are among the top 30 breeds registered by the American Kennel Club, and their popularity is rising. In 2007, the Mastiff ranked 28th among AKC-registered breeds, and 2,328 litters were registered in 2006. Before you decide to cash in on that popularity by breeding your Mastiff, ask yourself whether you have the time, energy, and money to deal with six or more active, curious, giant-breed puppies that will grow quickly, eat a lot, and trample through your home. The costs of breeding a Mastiff include veterinary specialist expenses for obtaining four or more health certifications, the stud fee, the cost of shipping your bitch to the stud and then retrieving her, top-quality nutrition during the pregnancy, 10 to 12 weeks of raising a litter of puppies that can range from one to a dozen or more, and placing the pups into qualified homes.

Choose a Mastiff puppy who is friendly toward children, never shy.

of the risk of serious uterine infections in females and testicular cancer in males. In giant breeds such as the Mastiff, however, spay/neuter surgery before puberty can pose other health risks. These include a greater likelihood of cranial cruciate ligament ruptures, a common problem in dogs. Veterinarians often recommend that pet puppies be spayed or neutered at 4 to 6 months of age, but there is no scientific basis for that recommendation. In the case of a Mastiff, waiting until the dog has reached physical maturity at 18 to 36 months of age may be better.

There's an old wives' tale that altered dogs get fat, but it's just that—a tale. What really

white on any other part of the body, is a fault (see Official Mastiff Standard, page 59). The muzzle, nose, and ears are dark, the blacker the better, giving the Mastiff the appearance of wearing a mask.

Getting Papers

When you take your Mastiff puppy home, the breeder will present you with an AKC application form, which is filled out with the breed, sex, and color of the dog, the dog's date of birth, the registered names of the dog's sire and dam, and the breeder's name. To register the dog, complete the form with your name and address and the name you have chosen to register the dog under, and send it to the AKC with the proper fee. You can also register your puppy online at the AKC's web site: *www.akc.org.* You can also register your puppy online at the AKC's web site: *www.akc.org.* After the application is processed, you will be mailed an AKC registration certificate.

Some breeders withhold the registration form until the puppy has been spayed or neutered. Others use what is called a limited registration, meaning that your puppy can be registered, but none of its offspring can. Although dogs with limited registration cannot be shown in Conformation, they can take part in performance events such as Agility, Freestyle, Obedience, Rally Obedience, and Tracking. The upbeat, less-structured atmosphere of Rally Obedience makes it an especially good event for Mastiff participation. Many Mastiffs excel at Rally Obedience and have earned titles in this fun canine sport. Breeders often use the limited registration when they are not sure of a pup's potential as

happens is that the pup's metabolism starts to slow to the adult rate right around the time of puberty. Unless his diet and exercise level are adjusted, the dog will indeed gain weight, but not because of the spay/neuter surgery.

Which Color?

Mastiffs come in three colors: fawn, apricot, or brindle. A Mastiff with a brindle coat should have a fawn or apricot background that is completely covered with dark stripes. Occasionally there is a small patch of white on the chest, but too much white on the chest, or

Good Mastiff Names

Males

Alston: Old English, meaning noble stone
Arthur: Welsh, meaning bear
Bailey: Old French, meaning bailiff or keeper
Baskerville: after the giant hound of
  Sherlock Holmes fame
Carey: Old Welsh, meaning dweller of castles
Duff: Celtic, meaning dark-faced one
Edmund: Old English, meaning defender
  of property
Max: Latin, meaning greatest
Thane: Old English, meaning warrior
  attendant
William: Old High German, meaning resolute
  protector

Females

Cara: Gaelic, meaning friend
Damaris: Greek, meaning gentle
Delilah: Hebrew, meaning temptress
Elsa: Old German, meaning noble one
Hilda: Old German, meaning battle maid
Megan: Greek, meaning mighty one
Petra: Greek, meaning the rock
Sophie: Greek, meaning the wise
Thora: Old Norse, meaning thunder

Other paperwork the breeder should provide include the pup's veterinary records. A careful breeder will also give you a packet of information regarding the food your puppy has been eating, how often he is used to being fed, and other advice that will help the two of you make a smooth adjustment to living together.

Finally, consider the costs of caring for a giant-breed dog before purchasing a Mastiff puppy. Expenses you'll shell out for include extra-large bedding, bowls and collars as well as higher doses of medication for this super-size dog.

Acquiring an Adult Mastiff

Not every Mastiff puppy goes to a happily-ever-after life. Sometimes he is placed with an inappropriate family, while in other cases the family situation changes. A move to a new home, divorce, illness, or death can all lead to a Mastiff being displaced from his home.

Each year, as many as 250 Mastiffs nationwide are turned in to Mastiff rescue groups or animal shelters, which must then find good homes for them. If you can give a Mastiff a good home and don't mind taking an adolescent or adult dog, adopting one from a rescue group may be a good way to go. Be sure to discuss thoroughly with rescue personnel why the dog was given up, to ensure that you will be able to provide the dog with a suitable environment and behavioral structure.

Adopting a Mastiff is an opportunity to make a difference in a dog's life, and you will find that your good deed brings returns many times over in the love and companionship the dog gives you. To find a Mastiff rescue group, see the listing on page 92.

a show or breeding animal. If the pup grows up to be a quality dog, and you and the breeder both agree he should be bred, the breeder can then change the limited registration to full registration.

The breeder may also give you a copy of your Mastiff's pedigree, which is a written record of the dog's ancestry for three or more generations. A pedigree has no legal standing, but it contains important information if you choose to breed your dog.

BRINGING UP PUPPY

Once you've purchased the necessary puppy paraphernalia, turn your attention to socialization, housetraining, and good canine manners. Although they tend to be gentle and sedate, Mastiffs require training just like any other dog.

Shopping List

Knowing what to expect from your dog and being ready for any contingency puts you at the head of the puppy-owner pack, so put together a puppy kit before you bring home your new family member. You'll need to buy a collar, identification tag, leash, food, feeding dishes, crate, and toys.

Collar

Before setting off on your shopping spree, call the breeder and ask a few questions, starting with your pup's collar size. Select a flat buckle-style collar that can be adjusted as your puppy grows. To test the collar's fit, make sure you can slip two fingers between the collar and Samson's neck.

Samson should wear a choke-type training collar only when he is being trained and is under supervision. Faster than a Mastiff can pin a prowler, this type of collar can get hung up on something and choke the dog.

Identification Tag and Leash

Order an identification tag, even if you haven't decided your pup's name yet. Engrave it with your name, address, and phone number. Before you leave the breeder's, put the collar and tag on the pup. A nylon or leather leash will help you keep the puppy under control in its new surroundings.

Food

Ask the breeder what the puppy has been eating, and follow the breeder's recommendations for an appropriate diet. Not all foods are appropriate for Mastiffs. Let the breeder's experience guide you. If you choose to feed a different diet, gradually mix it in with the food the puppy is used to eating. Whatever food you choose, be sure it is labeled complete and balanced, with high-quality ingredients, and is formulated for puppy growth. You may want to purchase a food made for large-breed puppies. These diets are formulated to prevent the puppy from growing too quickly and from putting on too much weight, which can damage the still-developing musculoskeletal system. You may want to purchase a food made for large-breed puppies.

Food and Water Dishes

Of course, you'll also need a set of food and water dishes. Choose metal or ceramic dishes, not plastic. Metal dishes are handy because they can withstand being batted around and chewed on by a puppy, and they're easy to clean. Ceramic dishes are good, especially for holding water, because they're heavy, making them difficult to tip over. Avoid plastic dishes, which can be chewed up and swallowed by your Mastiff, causing an obstruction. Dogs can also develop allergies to plastic dishes, which can lead to staph infections of the chin area. Whatever you choose, buy the 5-quart (4.7 L) size; your puppy will soon grow into it.

Mastiffs tend to be messy eaters, and food can get trapped in their jowls. Keep a towel handy for face-washing after each meal.

Crate

A crate is one of the most important purchases you will make. It allows your puppy to ride safely in the car, gives the pup a place where he can feel secure, and is a super house-training tool. The crate can be made of wire or plastic, depending on your needs. A typical crate size for a full-grown Mastiff is 54 inches (137 cm) by 37 inches (94 cm) by 45 inches (114 cm). A wire crate offers good ventilation and folds up for storage. Full-grown male Mastiffs may have difficulty entering even the largest plastic crate, so for home use a wire crate may be the best choice. A plastic crate is necessary if your dog will be traveling by air. In addition, puppies may feel more secure in a plastic crate, since it is not open to view.

Toys

Last, but not least, be sure to buy a couple of toys to keep your Mastiff entertained and out of trouble. A good chew toy will distract your puppy from chewing on things he shouldn't. Choose toys that are sturdy, with no buttons or bells that can be chewed off and swallowed. Favorite Mastiff toys are large sterilized beef bones, Nylabones, large Kong toys, and rope bones. Any toy you give your Mastiff should be something large that he can't chew up easily. Throw away rope toys once they begin to unravel. With luck, Samson's Kongs and Nylabones will last about three months. For outdoor play, a tire in the yard will keep your Mastiff entertained, as will a log or two. Both are items that he can pick up and drag around to his heart's content. Like other dogs, Mastiffs enjoy playing with balls, but they need something a little larger than a tennis ball, which they will peel very quickly. Try a basketball or soccer ball.

Puppy-proofing

With any puppy it's important to make the home environment safe, but a Mastiff puppy is a special challenge. These dogs love to chew, and they can do a great deal of damage in a very small amount of time. Many Mastiff puppies have died or been injured from eating socks and pantyhose that caused intestinal obstructions. Others are rock eaters and can down 2 or 3 pounds (0.9–1.4 kg) of them in a brief 10 or 15 minutes.

With this in mind, take extra-special care to puppy-proof your home and yard:

✔ Use child safety locks on kitchen and bathroom cabinets that contain cleansers and medications.

✔ Keep garbage out of reach or in an area that is off limits to your puppy. Using a trash compactor is even better, as long as you are always careful to keep the door closed.

✔ Wrap up electrical cords so they are less noticeable to a pup's roving eye, and coat cords with Bitter Apple or some other nasty substance that will deter them from chewing.

✔ Put rat bait or other poisonous substances such as antifreeze in locked cabinets in the garage. For even greater safety, buy antifreeze that contains the less toxic propylene glycol rather than ethylene glycol.

✔ Take note of your house plants and landscaping. Many common house and yard plants are toxic to dogs. These include caladium; dieffenbachia, or dumb cane;

elephant's ear; and philodendron. Other plants with toxic properties include bulbs such as amaryllis, daffodils, hyacinth, iris, jonquils and narcissus; and azaleas, English ivy, holly berries, hydrangea, jasmine, ligustrum and privet hedges, oleander, and wisteria. If you have any of these plants, put them out of the dog's reach, isolate them with some type of barrier, or build a run for your dog in a safe area of the yard.

Never assume that your Mastiff can't or won't get into something. Get down on your hands and knees and explore your house at puppy level to make sure you haven't missed any potential dangers.

Feeding Your Puppy

Mastiff puppies grow at a dramatic rate, but it's important not to push their growth—bigger is not better. If your Mastiff grows too quickly or puts on too much weight, bone and joint problems can result. For the same reason, avoid giving calcium supplements.

Discuss the best food for your pup with your veterinarian, and take the pup in regularly to be weighed. (Most veterinarians don't charge fees just for weighing the dog.) Mastiff puppies usually eat three to four times daily until they are six to nine months old. Start cutting back meals when your dog shows less interest in the midday meal.

Dogs like a routine, and Mastiffs are especially likely to become set in their ways, showing great displeasure when a meal or some other regular event does not occur on time. Your Mastiff will do best when you feed him at the same time and in the same place every day. Feeding your Mastiff on a regular sched-

itself. Avoid switching foods frequently. Sudden changes in diet can cause intestinal upset, and your dog may also develop picky eating habits.

After your Mastiff finishes eating, put him in his crate to rest. Heavy exercise and drinking too much water after eating are frequently linked to gastric torsion, a potentially fatal condition.

Outdoor Shelter

Despite its great size, the Mastiff is a house dog and should not live solely outdoors. A Mastiff who is tied outside or chained with little human interaction becomes neurotic at best, aggressive at worst. Nonetheless, there are times when your Mastiff must be outside, and a good, sturdy doghouse is a must to protect him from the elements. Doghouses come in many shapes and styles, and can be made of wood or plastic. With the Mastiff's propensity for chewing, plastic may be the better choice. The doghouse should be large enough for your Mastiff to stand up, turn around, and lie down in comfortably. Place the doghouse in an area that offers plenty of shade. Ideally, it will face south or east for protection from cold north winds.

If possible, provide your Mastiff with a pen or run in the yard to keep him safe from poisonous plants or other hazards. A good size is 10 feet by 30 feet (3–9 m) or larger. Gravel is the best ground cover for a Mastiff's pen. It's good for the dog's feet, and it's small enough to pass through the digestive tract if swallowed.

The Mastiff is generally a homebody, unlikely to roam, but a fenced yard is a must for any breed, especially one with the territorial instincts of the Mastiff. A fence will protect

ule also assists with house-training, making it easier to predict when the puppy needs to eliminate. Feed your dog in a quiet place where there isn't a lot of coming and going, and wait to feed it if it has been exerting

Age and Weight Chart

8 weeks	16 to 18 pounds (7.3–8.2 kg)
12 weeks	32 to 34 pounds (14.5–15.4 kg)
16 weeks	50 to 52 pounds (22.7–23.6 kg)
6 months	88 to 90 pounds (40.0–40.9 kg)
9 months	130 to 140 pounds (59.0–63.6 kg)
1 year	140 to more than 200 pounds (63.6–90.8 kg)

After your dog eliminates, let him have some time to sniff, dig, and play.

your dog from traffic and prevent him from attempting to expand his territory to neighbors' yards. He will bark at people and other dogs going by, and they will no doubt feel safer with a fence between them and your gentle giant.

The ideal choice is a 6-foot (1.8 m) wooden fence. A solid barrier such as this keeps children from teasing the dog, and lessens territorial behavior such as barking when people go by. Mastiffs are not big jumpers, so if need be you can get by with a 4- or 5-foot (1.2–1.6 m) fence. The only problem you might face is damage to the fence if your Mastiff takes to leaning or jumping against it. This is something you can teach your pup not to do, however, and it's a lesson that should be learned early, before the dog is big enough to do any damage.

Housetraining

Mastiffs are fastidious, observant, and eager to please, making them easily house-trained. If they are taken out regularly to eliminate or have an older dog to learn from, they can be housetrained in as little as three days. However, they are not physiologically mature enough to hold their urine for long periods until they are four to six months old, so trustworthy housetraining is not possible until then.

As with any type of training, consistency is the key. Take your pup out several times a day to eliminate. This elimination schedule should take place as nearly as possible at the same time each day. A typical schedule might be first thing in the morning after waking, immediately after each meal or after drinking, after playtime, and just before bedtime.

Always take your puppy out on a leash to eliminate. This accomplishes two things: It allows you to be sure the pup urinated and defecated, and it helps the puppy form an association between going out and eliminating. Praise Samson as he eliminates. Again, this creates pleasant associations for him. After he has done his business, spend a few minutes playing, then take him inside and place him in his crate to rest.

When it comes to housetraining, the crate can be a puppy owner's best friend. Dogs are den animals, and they are conditioned not to soil their den, or sleeping, areas. By putting Samson in the crate when you can't supervise him, you prevent accidents in the house. This is good for you, because you don't have to clean them up, and good for Samson, because he doesn't get scolded for making a mistake. Whenever possible, you should make sure your Mastiff only has opportunities to do the right thing. That will make life easier for both of you.

In the House

A crate is also useful for keeping a puppy out of harm's way and protecting your clothes, shoes, furniture, and other household items from sharp puppy teeth. Make it a habit to put your puppy in the crate whenever you can't keep an eye on him. The crate is not a place of punishment; rather, it's a place of rest where your pup can't get into trouble and won't be bothered by inquisitive children or other pets.

The idea, however, is not to isolate your Mastiff. Keep the crate in an area where there's plenty of family activity, such as the den or kitchen. Remind children that the crate is off limits when the puppy is inside—no banging on the top or poking fingers inside.

At night, the puppy can sleep in the crate in your bedroom. Your presence will be reassuring, especially to a pack animal like the Mastiff. Also, you'll be right there to take the puppy out when you first hear him stirring in the morning.

Except overnight or on an airplane flight, never leave your puppy or adult dog in a crate for more than four hours at a time. Puppies can't control their bladders for much longer than that, and no dog should be kept confined for long periods without companionship or exercise.

You can also use a wire mesh baby gate or exercise pen to confine your dog to an area such as the kitchen, bathroom, or laundry room. There's a little more room for Samson to explore, and the tile or linoleum floors are easy to clean if he has an accident. Of course, you'll want to make sure the room is puppy-proofed first.

Leash Training

On-leash activity is the safest way for your Mastiff to exercise in an open area. Walking a Mastiff on a leash is an experience. While your dog enjoys your company, he's also curious about what's up ahead, and his powerful tug on the leash can make you feel as if your arm is coming out of its socket. Begin teaching your Mastiff puppy right away not to pull on the leash. You have only a small window of opportunity before your Mastiff weighs as much as or more than you do.

Accustom your puppy to the leash from day one. Let him wear the leash around the house, dragging it behind. Your puppy may twist and turn, trying to rid himself of the strange new "tail," but that's perfectly normal. Let the pup get used to the leash at his own pace. When he stops fighting with the leash, call him and

Teach your Mastiff to walk nicely on leash before he becomes big enough to drag you around the block.

reward him with praise and a treat if he comes to you. The puppy will learn to associate wearing the leash with good things.

Next, encourage the puppy to follow you while you're holding the leash. Hold it loose and low, and call the puppy as you walk forward. Again, give praise and a treat if the pup complies. Practice walking with the leash for a few minutes several times a day, and always make it fun. Stop before the puppy gets bored or frustrated. In puppy kindergarten, your Mastiff will get more practice in walking on a leash.

Trainer Brian Kilcommons emphasizes the importance of letting your dog "ask questions"

about leash training. Keep the leash loose so the puppy can experiment with what's allowed and what's not. If the pup pulls, correct him. Praise him when he walks nicely without pulling.

Because of their great size, Mastiffs almost can't help pulling. A good compromise might be to use a retractable leash, which allows your dog to range out to 16 feet (4.8 m). If this is not an option, try using a head collar to keep pulling to a minimum. A head collar resembles a horse halter and works on the principle that by controlling the head, you control the rest of the body. Used correctly, it is a safe, gentle method of keeping your dog under control. Harnesses, unlike head halters, may offer little control and encourage the dog to pull. Others, though, are designed to help prevent pulling. Talk to a trainer about the best option for your Mastiff.

Riding in the Car

It's always nice to have a dog that rides well in the car. Trips to the veterinarian go much easier when Samson isn't throwing himself all around the car or loudly throwing up in the backseat. And for a Mastiff who competes in conformation or performance events, frequent car travel is essential. So are good car manners.

Most Mastiffs enjoy riding in the car and will sit quietly and look out the window. As with anything else, though, that kind of behavior happens only when it is learned at an early age. The polite Mastiff respects your authority and learns to wait until you give the okay before jumping in or out of the car. For greatest safety, your dog should ride in a crate. If you must stop suddenly, you don't want 175 pounds (79 kg) of Mastiff flying through the windshield.

To accustom Samson to riding in the car, take him on brief errands to the bank or post office. If he is lucky, the drive-up bank teller will give him a biscuit. As with any other type of training, praise the dog for riding nicely and correct him when he misbehaves. Woofing along with you to the music on the radio is okay; nonstop barking or hanging his head out the window isn't.

Warning: It's unwise to leave your Mastiff alone in the car. You risk the dog overheating on a warm day, even if you roll the windows down, and you risk having your car destroyed by a bored dog, unless he's confined to a crate. Mastiffs can also be territorial about their cars and may bark or even bite if people approach the car or reach in to pet them.

Puppy Kindergarten

Forget you ever heard that old wives tale about waiting until a dog is six months old to train him. By that time, your Mastiff will be huge and well on his way to running the household. Early training in puppy kindergarten, beginning when the pup is 9 to 12 weeks old, is highly recommended. Your breeder may be able to refer you to a class run by the local dog club, or one may be offered by your veterinarian.

The good manners your puppy will learn in kindergarten include the commands sit, stay, down, and come. The pup will also learn to walk nicely on a leash and accept handling for grooming and veterinary exams. You will learn the basics of house-training and problem prevention, the best ways to motivate your puppy,

Avoid leaving your Mastiff alone in the car. He could overheat, even if it doesn't seem excessively hot outdoors.

and how to time rewards and corrections so they are effective. Socialization is another aspect of puppy kindergarten. Your Mastiff will meet lots of new dogs and people there, and you'll play fun games like "Pass the Puppy" so all the dogs become accustomed to being petted and handled by other people.

Before you start a class, ask the trainer which breeds he or she has had experience with. Mastiffs are highly sensitive and respond well to calm, positive training methods. Harsh or physically rough treatment is unnecessary and can even damage your blossoming relationship with the dog.

A puppy kindergarten class can also help you spot problems in the making. The trainer may recognize possessive or territorial traits in your dog that you hadn't noticed. Professional help at this early stage can give your dog a needed attitude adjustment before it's too big to control.

Visiting the Veterinarian

Because Mastiffs are not common, this may be your veterinarian's first experience with one. Samson's first visit to the veterinarian should be a positive experience. He will receive a thorough physical exam and any booster vaccinations needed to fight off the infectious diseases that threaten dogs: parvovirus, distemper, and adenovirus-2. At four months of age, he will need to be vaccinated against rabies.

A fecal exam is also a good idea. Bring a fresh stool sample so the veterinarian can examine it for signs of internal parasites such as roundworms, tapeworms, hookworms, and whipworms (see pages 88–89).

While the veterinarian examines your puppy, take this opportunity to ask for advice on

dental care, grooming (especially nail trimming), nutrition, and spaying and neutering. You might also ask the veterinarian to explain emergency or first aid procedures in case your Mastiff swallows and chokes on an object or eats something poisonous. Be sure you know what number to call for after-hours emergencies and where the nearest emergency clinic is located.

Vaccination Chart

Canine Parvovirus: First vaccination at 6 to 8 weeks of age and then every 3 to 4 weeks after, with final vaccination given no sooner than 16 weeks. Booster at 1 year. Revaccination recommended every three years thereafter. Special circumstances may warrant vaccination more or less frequently.

Distemper virus: First vaccination at 6 to 8 weeks of age and then every 3 to 4 weeks after, with final vaccination given no sooner than 16 weeks. Booster at 1 year. Revaccination recommended every three years thereafter. Special circumstances may warrant vaccination more or less frequently.

Adenovirus–2: First vaccination at 6 to 8 weeks of age and then every 3 to 4 weeks after, with final vaccination given no sooner than 16 weeks. Booster at 1 year. Revaccination recommended every three years thereafter. Special circumstances may warrant vaccination more or less frequently.

Rabies: First vaccination at 16 weeks of age, with booster at 1 year of age. Triennial (every three years) vaccinations follow thereafter or as required by law.*

*Some states require rabies vaccinations annually or biennially (every two years).

Start leash training early.

If a puppy class isn't available in your area, you can still teach proper canine etiquette to your Mastiff at home. Besides leash training, a puppy needs to know the commands for *sit, down, stay,* and *come.* They are the foundation of a well-trained dog that you can take anywhere.

"Sit"

Sit is one of the easiest commands to teach. Get your puppy's attention, show him a treat, and then raise the treat directly above his head. The puppy will naturally move into a sitting position.

When he does, say *"Sit"* and give the treat. Practice this for a couple of minutes several times a day. Your dog will soon associate the word *sit* with the action of sitting (and receiving a treat). Once the puppy is sitting consistently on command, scale back the treats to every other *sit,* and then to every three or four *sits.* Eventually, you can phase out the treats and offer praise instead.

"Down"

Once your pup has learned to sit, you can introduce the command for *down.* The *down* command comes in especially handy when your

Mastiff is standing in front of the television set, blocking your view. To teach the *down* command, first put the pup in a *sit.* Then show a treat, moving it down and forward until it is in front of the puppy's paws. The puppy should move naturally into the *down* position. When he does, say *"Down"* and reward him with the treat. Practice this the same way you did for the *sit* command.

Note: The trick with these first two commands is not to confuse your dog. Use only the words *sit* and *down.* Don't tell your dog to *"Sit down"* or *"Lie down"* or he won't know what you're talking about.

Sit is one of the easiest commands to teach.

For the same reason, if the dog jumps up on you or on a forbidden piece of furniture, say *"Off,"* not *"Down."*

"Stay"

Next, teach your puppy to stay in a sitting or *down* position. It's probably easiest to start with the *down* position. Put a leash on the dog so you can control his actions. Standing in front of him, lean over, say *"Down,"* then put your hand, palm forward, in front of his face and say *"Stay."* Stand up and step back a few paces. Don't rush, and don't go too slowly. Remain there for only a few seconds, and return to the dog. As you do, put your foot on the leash so the pup can't get up. Praise the pup for staying, and then give a release command such as *"okay"* to indicate that he can get up.

If your dog gets up after you've told him to stay, simply place him back in the *down* position without scolding and start over. Patience is a must.

Gradually increase the distance you go and length of time you stay. Aim for a ten-minute *stay,* and take plenty of time to get there. Always give lots of praise before releasing the dog from the *stay.* Once your dog has learned to stay while lying down, you can link the *stay* and *sit* commands.

"Come"

The most important command any dog can know is the one for *come.* Make the act of coming to you as pleasant and enticing as possible. Rattle a box of treats to get your dog's attention, and say *"Samson, come!"* Use a happy, excited tone of voice. When he responds, heap on the praise and treats.

Make teaching "Come!" a pleasant experience.

Once you've established that coming to your call is well worth the effort, teaching this command can take a more formal turn. Attach a 20- to 30-foot (6.1–9.1 m) clothesline to Samson's collar and start running away from him, feeding out the line as you go. Don't let the line get tight. When you get a good distance away, call him to you. If he responds, keep backing away while encouraging him to follow you. If he doesn't respond, use the line to draw him toward you, still praising him for coming. Use this technique only once per training session. Save a repeat for another day.

Never use the *come* command to call your dog for something unpleasant such as a scolding or being given a pill. That's the quickest way to teach a dog *not* to come.

Remember, puppies have brief attention spans, so keep training sessions short, and always end them when your dog has been successful, not after a correction.

Grooming is essential. It promotes healthy skin and coat and good dental hygiene. It also helps to prevent ear infections, itchy skin problems, and broken toenails or damaged foot pads.

Coat Care

Grooming a Mastiff is pretty simple. The short coat is easy to brush, and the only other work needed is regular nail trimming, ear cleaning, and dental care. Bathing is necessary only when the dog is dirty.

Start getting your Mastiff used to being groomed as soon as you take him home. Even a squirmy puppy can learn to sit still for a few minutes while being brushed and having his eyes and ears cleaned.

Brushing

Regular brushing is the foundation of the grooming process. Using a rubber hound glove, which can be purchased at a pet supply store, brush your Mastiff weekly or even daily. Brushing removes loose hair and dead skin cells, distributes skin oils, and helps keep the coat shiny. It feels good, too, and your dog will soon come to enjoy being brushed. Avoid brushes with long or sharp bristles, such as pin brushes or wire slicker brushes. During the shedding season, which takes place twice a year in the spring and fall, a terrier stripping blade can come in handy to remove loose hair. Some Mastiffs shed only during this time, while others shed heavily throughout the year. There's no way to predict which kind you'll get.

Giving a Bath

It's rare that a Mastiff needs a bath. Only if Samson is exceptionally dirty or is competing in a dog show should he require bathing. Your puppy can be bathed in the tub, of course, but it won't be long before he outgrows it. Then you'll probably need to give baths out in the yard, using the hose. Fortunately, Mastiffs often enjoy water and will stand quite happily for a bath. There will be lots of shaking of big wet dog going on, so wear old clothes that you don't mind getting wet. Gather your supplies before you begin the bath.

You'll need plenty of towels, cotton balls to place in the ears to keep the water out, and a shampoo made for dogs.

1. Wet Samson thoroughly with warm water, then lather, starting at the head and working your way to the tail.
2. Rinse well, since leftover soap on the skin can be irritating. A vinegar rinse (1 part cider

vinegar to 1 part water) can help ensure that you get all the soap out of the coat.

3. Soak up as much water from the coat as possible, and towel-dry Samson thoroughly. Unless the weather is very warm, don't let him air dry outside, and keep him out of cold or drafty areas until he's completely dry. (This is a good time for him to be in his crate.) Put a sweatshirt on Samson or wrap a blanket around him to keep him warm while he dries. Consider using a forced-air dryer to get him completely dry in a timely manner.

Coat and Skin Problems

The skin is the body's largest external organ and serves as a barrier, protecting the body from injury, preventing loss of water and electrolytes, and preserving body heat. It secretes oils that protect the coat and have antibacterial properties, and it plays a role in the production of vitamin D. The skin is a sensory organ as well, allowing the experiences of touch, temperature, and pain.

Making up the skin are two layers, the epidermis, or outer layer, which is protected by the hair, and the dermis, or inner layer, which nourishes and supports the epidermis. The surface of the skin is colonized by numerous bacteria that generally live there peacefully, never causing a problem. Trouble begins when a break in the skin provides the bacteria access to deeper layers or permits a greater than normal accumulation of bacteria.

Skin problems in Mastiffs can be frustrating. The most important step is to seek out underlying problems since they often affect the skin and must be treated as well.

Pyoderma

Probably the most common skin condition in Mastiffs is pyoderma, a cutaneous bacterial infection that is usually caused by *Staphylococcus intermedius,* one of the bacteria that normally live on a dog's skin. Pyoderma is frequently a sign of an underlying health problem such as hypothyroidism.

In Mastiffs, pyoderma usually manifests itself in small black crusty lesions on the back and the back of the neck. The hair in these areas is easily pulled out and feels oily or dirty. The dog is itchy, thanks to the production of inflammatory toxins and enzymes by the bacteria, and its skin may smell bad. In some cases, circles of crusty lesions are found on the groin and abdomen, or the hair on the flanks thins and the skin becomes dark. Not surprisingly, a Mastiff with pyoderma is pretty miserable.

Diagnosis of skin problems is often a long process of elimination. Be prepared to tell your veterinarian when the signs first appeared, whether the dog is itchy, what the dog eats, and what the environmental conditions are like: Is your garden in bloom or have you recently replaced the carpet in the house? Anything you can tell the veterinarian will be helpful. Diagnostic techniques may include any or all of the following: a complete blood count, a full blood profile, a chemistry panel, a thyroid panel, skin scrapings, fungal cultures, and a urinalysis. The veterinarian may also culture the skin lesions and examine them under a microscope to determine the bacterial population.

Once pyoderma has been diagnosed, treatment usually requires a lengthy course of antibiotics, plus thyroid medication if that is indicated. Generally, the antibiotics should be continued for at least one week after the problem appears to be resolved. Thyroid medication usually is continued for the rest of the dog's life. Shampoos containing benzoyl peroxide or chlorhexadine can also be helpful, working to restore a normal environment on the skin's surface and removing crusts, scales, and other surface debris.

Dental Care

To keep Samson's mouth healthy, brush his teeth regularly. Brushing prevents the formation of plaque and tartar, and keeps bacteria from multiplying and causing infection. For best results, brushing should be done daily, but even a weekly brushing is better than nothing. Use a soft toothbrush and a toothpaste made for dogs (toothpaste made for humans can cause stomach upset in dogs).

Eyes and Ears

Keep the corners of the eyes free of dried mucus, and the ears dry and clean. One way to do this is to wipe the ears out with witch hazel every week to remove dust and dirt. Another solution that can be used to clean ears is three parts alcohol mixed with one part white vinegar. Used two or three times a week, this mixture creates an acid environment that helps prevent the growth of yeasts and most bacteria.

Keep an eye out for sticky seeds, ear mites, or signs of infection, such as redness, tenderness, or the dog shaking its head frequently or pawing at its ears (see page 77 for more about treatment of ear infections). Ear infections in Mastiffs can be long-lasting, requiring treatment with systemic antibiotics to clear them up.

Nail Care

It is most important to keep the nails well trimmed. Mastiffs are sensitive about their feet, and Samson will probably act as if you are killing him when you trim him nails, but don't let him fool you. When done properly and often, nail trimming doesn't hurt and is an important part of keeping the dog's feet healthy. Use a large nail trimmer made for dogs, and clip just at the curve of the nail. If the nails are light-colored or clear, you can see the dark line of the quick. Avoid nicking it, because that is painful and can cause the nail to bleed. Keep some Quik-Stop or cornstarch handy to stop the bleeding if you make a mistake while trimming.

Mastiff owners have many high-quality options for feeding their dogs, including specially formulated growth diets for large and giant breeds. These foods help prevent puppies from growing too quickly and stressing their still developing musculoskeletal systems.

Feeding Your Mastiff

"Holy cow!" most people say when they see a Mastiff. "How much food does that dog eat?" The answer is quite a bit during the first year, but about the same as any other large dog when full-grown. That ranges from four to eight cups of food daily, depending on the dog's size, activity level, and the type of food being given.

Food is the fuel that keeps the Mastiff's massive body operating. The components of food are protein, fat, carbohydrates, vitamins, and minerals. Protein, which is made up of smaller units called amino acids, builds strong muscles and connective tissue such as hair, skin, cartilage, ligaments, and tendons, and it's critical for an effective immune system. Fat cushions the vital organs and is a highly digestible source of energy. Carbohydrates also provide energy, as well as fiber for proper function of the gastrointestinal tract, and they are essential in the formation of certain amino acids and other body compounds and tissues. Vitamins and minerals, although they are present only in tiny amounts, are needed by the body to carry out a number of metabolic processes.

Choosing a Food

It's clear, then, that the choice of food can profoundly affect a Mastiff's well-being. A diet that is complete and balanced provides just the right mix of all these substances to meet a dog's needs. Pet food formulation is governed by the American Association of Feed Control Officials (AAFCO), which decides the minimum and maximum requirements for a food to be labeled nutritionally adequate. Manufacturers of pet food spend millions of dollars each year studying the nutritional needs of dogs, and developing and testing formulas.

The most effective way of testing a food is through feeding trials, in which a number of dogs are fed the diet over an extended period. Researchers make careful observations about the dogs' physical response to the food—overall health, coat condition, type and amount of feces produced—and whether the dogs like the food. After all, the best food in the world can't do much good if a dog won't eat it!

Reading Labels

Manufacturers may also test a food's nutritional value through chemical analysis, but this is a much less precise method than feeding trials. The label is required to state how a food's nutritional value was determined, and you are better off selecting one whose claims include the terms "complete and balanced," "feeding tests," "AAFCO feeding test protocols" or "AAFCO feeding studies."

The label will also indicate the life stage for which the food is formulated, such as puppies, adults, or aging dogs. Dogs have different nutritional needs at different times in their lives. Puppyhood is a time of rapid growth, but large and giant breeds that grow too quickly can develop crippling bone and joint disorders. Don't let your Mastiff puppy gain too much weight. Your veterinarian and the breeder can advise you when to switch your Mastiff from a puppy food to an adult maintenance food. Some fast-growing puppies may begin eating a maintenance diet as early as eight weeks of age, but others can wait until they are six months to one year old.

Ingredient List in Labels

As you evaluate foods, be sure you understand how to read an ingredient list. Ingredients are listed by weight, in decreasing order. In other words, if chicken is the first ingredient listed, there is more chicken in the food than any other ingredient. Sometimes, different forms of the same ingredient are listed separately—for instance, ground rice, rice flour, and rice bran—so there may be more of a certain ingredient than it appears at first glance. Take these "split ingredients" into account when you're evaluating the makeup of a food.

Ideally, a food will contain high-quality sources of protein, such as beef, lamb, or poultry. The food you choose should list two or more meat ingredients at or near the beginning of the ingredients list. Look for specific types of meat—chicken, beef, or lamb—rather than the generic term *meat*, which could be from any animal source. Animal-based protein is more digestible. In other words, the dog's body can make better use of animal-based protein than of grain-based protein. A food's digestibility level is not included on the label, but you can gauge it yourself by observing your dog's condition. Is the coat shiny? Does the dog produce relatively small, firm feces? If your answer to these questions is yes, you can be assured that the food you're giving contains high-quality ingredients that meet your dog's needs.

Palatability and Price

Does your dog like the taste of his food? Palatability is an important concern. Dogs are individuals, and they have individual tastes and nutritional needs. A good food that suits one dog may not suit another.

There's also the question of canned versus dry. Each type has advantages and disadvantages. Naturally, most dogs find canned food more tasty than dry food, but canned food, once opened, spoils more quickly, is messy, and has an odor that isn't very appealing to people, although dogs seem to like it just fine. Dry food is less expensive and has a longer shelf life. Both canned and dry foods can provide high-quality nutrition, so make the choice after weighing your own preferences as well as the dog's. For the best of both worlds, you can always feed both.

Choices in dog foods go beyond canned and dry these days. Alternatives include high-quality commercial raw and dehydrated diets and homemade food formulated for dogs. Any

You can judge a food's quality by how well your Mastiff reacts to it. He should have a healthy coat, clear eyes, an alert attitude, and a normal activity level.

of these dietary choices can provide your Mastiff with excellent nutrition if fed properly. If you choose to go the homemade route, consult a veterinary nutritionist to ensure that what you are feeding to your Mastiff is complete and balanced.

Another aspect of choosing a food is price. Unless you're independently wealthy, price will matter, but it shouldn't be the determining factor. You will save more money in the long run by feeding a high-quality food than by buying whatever's on sale or rock-bottom-price generic brands. Choose one brand that meets your dog's needs and is priced for your budget, and stick to it. To determine how much it costs to feed a certain brand each day, write the price on your calendar the day you start feeding him and track how long it lasts. Divide the cost by the number of days to get the cost per day; for instance, if a bag of food costs $45 and lasts for ten days, its cost per day is $4.50.

Finally, take into account the manufacturer's responsiveness to consumers. Check the label for a toll-free number you can call if you have questions about ingredients, digestibility, or any other facet of dog nutrition.

Water

Water is also a vital part of your dog's diet. Keep plenty of fresh water available for your dog. Adult Mastiffs can drink as much as several gallons a day.

Should You Give Supplements?

With our society's emphasis on fitness and nutrition, it's natural to be concerned about

and giant breeds such as Mastiffs. Unless your veterinarian recommends a supplement for a specific condition, avoid adding one to your dog's diet.

Nutritional No-Nos

Like many dogs, Mastiffs will eat just about anything—and they're the perfect height for counter-surfing—but that doesn't mean they should. Avoid giving your Mastiff table scraps, bones from cooked poultry, and toxic substances such as alcohol and chocolate.

Chocolate in large amounts is toxic to dogs. It contains a chemical called theobromine to which dogs are unusually sensitive. Unsweetened baking chocolate has the highest amount of theobromine, but a dog that eats a box of chocolate candy or gets into a Halloween stash is likely to receive a large dose. Signs of chocolate toxicosis usually occur four or five hours after the dog eats the chocolate and include vomiting, diarrhea, panting, restlessness, and muscle tremors.

As for the other no-nos, table scraps are usually high in fat and only encourage the dog to beg at the table, a habit that should not be permitted. In addition, high-fat foods can cause serious cases of pancreatitis. If you feed a raw diet, use good food-handling practices. To prevent potential salmonella infection in yourself or your dog, wash your hands after handling raw meat. Always wash your Mastiff's dishes after each meal by using hot, soapy water and then rinsing thoroughly with hot water. Salmonella poisoning in dogs can cause vomiting and diarrhea, and is transmissible to people. The bones from fish, poultry, and pork can splinter easily and become lodged in the dog's throat. Like chocolate, alcohol can be

whether a beloved dog is getting the proper amount of vitamins and minerals in his diet. That's understandable, since so many of us are guilty of eating more junk food and fewer fruits and vegetables than we should. Our dogs, however, are lucky enough to have available foods that are specially formulated to provide them with all their nutritional needs. That being the case, most veterinary nutritionists recommend against adding supplements to a dog's diet. Too much of a good thing is just as bad as too little, and oversupplementation of vitamins and minerals, especially in puppyhood, can lead to skeletal disorders such as hip dysplasia, osteochondritis dissecans, and hypertrophic osteodystrophy. These conditions are most common in large toxic to dogs, and of course there is no reason to give it to them.

Healthy Treats

Some of the healthy treats that Mastiffs are fond of include crunchy vegetables, such as broccoli and carrots, and fresh fruit, including apples, bananas, and oranges. These are all low-calorie treats that you can give without a guilty conscience. Another good, low-calorie treat is plain popcorn with no butter or salt.

Keeping Your Mastiff Trim

Obesity is one of the most common health problems affecting dogs. A survey of veterinarians shows that as many as a quarter of their canine patients are overweight. Obesity puts a dog at risk for such chronic health problems as diabetes, heart disease, and arthritis because of the extra stress placed on the joints. However, you should limit exercise such as jumping and running on hard surfaces until a Mastiff puppy reaches physical maturity at 2 years of age.

Dogs are defined as obese when they weigh 20 percent or more above their normal weight. You can tell if Samson is too fat by giving him the hands-on test. First, place both thumbs on his backbone and spread your fingers along the rib cage. You should be able to feel the bony part of each rib beneath a slight layer of fat. As you stand over him, his waist should be visible behind the ribs and his abdomen tucked up behind the rib cage, giving him an hourglass figure. If Samson is shaped more like a can of dog food, he probably needs to go on a diet and get more exercise.

Before you make any changes in the dog's food or exercise level, take him to the veteri-

narian to make sure the excess weight doesn't have a medical cause, such as hypothyroidism. Once Samson has a clean bill of health, you and your veterinarian can develop a reducing plan that will let him lose weight safely. This may involve reducing the amount of food he receives or switching him to a low-calorie diet and gradually increasing the amount of

physical activity. Just as with people, it isn't good for dogs to lose too much weight at once. Start with three 20-minute walks each week, and gradually increase the length or frequency of the walks.

Weight-loss Tips

✔ Reduce the number of treats you give, and replace them with praise and play time, which have no calories at all.

✔ Use a measuring cup at feeding time so you don't give too much. Simply giving a level cup instead of a heaping cup will help reduce the amount of calories your dog consumes.

✔ Feed several small meals each day. Your dog will feel less deprived, and you'll reduce the possibility of bloat.

✔ Make sure everyone in the family understands that Samson is on a diet—no sneaking food to him on the side! To keep everyone honest, set up a chart to record who feeds the dog, including treats, how much, and when.

✔ Schedule regular weigh-ins at the veterinarian's office so you can track your progress.

✔ Don't expect overnight results. Slow and steady weight loss is safest and more long-lasting.

Eating the Wrong Thing

Household cleansers, rat poisons, yard treatments, and antifreeze can all cause poisoning in dogs. Something as simple as Samson lapping up a small spill of sweet-tasting antifreeze or walking through a treated yard and then licking his paws can lead to severe illness and even death.

Also toxic are seasonal plants such as Easter lilies, common household, yard, and garden plants such as azaleas, caladium, Dieffenbachia (dumbcane), English ivy (berries and leaves), ficus (leaves), holly, mistletoe (berries), oleander, and philodendron, and bulbs such as amaryllis, daffodil, iris, and tulip.

Indications that your dog has come into contact with something poisonous include drooling, vomiting, convulsing, muscle weakness, diarrhea, collapse, and coma. Sometimes the eyes, mouth, or skin become irritated.

Rapid, expert advice is vital. If veterinary care is not immediately available but you can identify the substance, call the National Animal Poison Control Center for advice. The phone number for the NAPCC is listed on page 92. If the poison is external, put on rubber gloves and wash the affected area with warm water. If you believe Samson has been poisoned by something he ate, give activated charcoal tablets to help adsorb the poison, binding it to the surface of the charcoal so it doesn't spread through the bloodstream. Do not induce vomiting unless advised to by the NAPCC or your veterinarian. Take the dog to your veterinarian as soon as possible. Be sure to bring the package containing the suspected poison and a sample of anything your dog has vomited. Rapid treatment is critical, especially if you believe Samson has ingested something as lethal as antifreeze or

Before you bring your puppy home, clear your yard of any plants with toxic properties that your Mastiff may nibble on. If you're not sure, contact a garden center for advice.

rat poison. It takes as little as two to four hours before he is beyond treatment.

Note: Keep a pet diary. A regular written record of Samson's condition and activity, as well as household events that could affect his health, can be a lifesaver. By knowing what's normal for your dog, and noting environmental changes that could affect him—having the house or yard treated for pests, planting bulbs in the garden, setting out rat bait—you are more likely to notice when something is wrong and to be able to trace the cause of the problem. Make it a habit to jot down your observations each day in a notebook or on your computer.

Begin teaching behavior basics as soon as you bring your puppy home at 10 to 12 weeks of age. Mastiffs are intelligent, but can sometimes be stubborn. Train them with patience and positive reinforcement.

Tips for Trainers

Your Mastiff is a sensitive dog who is intelligent and willing to please. Positive training techniques work best with this breed, which responds well to firm, consistent, kind training. Your Mastiff should certainly look to you as his leader, but physical punishment or cruelty are not necessary to establish your authority; they may even undermine your relationship with the dog. Mastiffs take it personally when you yell at them. A soft voice and praise are much more likely to get their attention. In most instances, a sharp "No" or clapped hands are as forceful as you'll need to get. Mastiffs are very tuned in to their people and quickly learn their likes and dislikes. Use the malleable puppy period to teach basic good manners. This foundation, plus a good share of patience and the knowledge that nothing is forever, will stand you in good stead during your Mastiff's adolescence.

Puberty for Mastiffs begins when they are about nine months old. During this "teenage" period, your young Mastiff may become a bit stubborn, testing your limits to see how far he can go.

The following tips will help you be successful in teaching your Mastiff everyday good manners.

✔ Give commands in a quiet tone of voice. That makes your dog pay attention to you.

✔ Be firm. Firmness is not the same as meanness or physical roughness. Firmness means using a deep tone of voice that commands attention and respect. It does not mean repeating a command several times until your dog finally complies. The dog must learn to pay attention the first time you speak, not to tune you out because you keep repeating the same thing over and over again. Never hit or shake your Mastiff, and avoid trainers who advocate harsh methods.

✔ Be consistent. Don't use the same words for different actions or combine two conflicting commands. Samson will only be confused when you tell him to *"Go sit down"* or say *"Get down"* when he jumps up on you. Use specific commands for each action, such as *"Sit," "Down,"* or *"Off."* Dogs can learn many different words and phrases.

✔ Develop a routine. Your dog will learn best if commands are phrased in the same way each time. When you're training, say the dog's name and give the command immediately before the action takes place. That way, Samson learns to comply as soon as he hears the proper sequence of words.

✔ Be patient. Mastiffs tend to develop slowly, both physically and emotionally. Don't be surprised if Samson still displays puppyish behavior when he is 18 months to 2 years old.

✔ Train when your dog is alert. Most of us just want to take a nap after we eat, and our dogs are the same way. Schedule training sessions before meals. Consider the weather as well; training in the heat of the day generally isn't a good idea.

✔ Understand the psychology behind positive reinforcement. Food treats and praise are tools that work only when used correctly. Hand them out lavishly when Samson is first learning, but increase your expectations and decrease the handouts as he becomes more proficient. So that he will always perform his best, Samson should never know when to expect a treat or praise. As an illustration, consider the difference between a vending machine and a slot machine. When we put 50 cents in a vending machine, we receive a package of corn chips and walk away. When we put 50 cents in a slot machine, sometimes we are rewarded with a payout and sometimes we're not, but the hope of hearing more quarters tumble out of the machine entices us into feeding more quarters into it. The hope of receiving a treat or praise will entice your dog into working harder for you.

✔ Keep training sessions brief and upbeat. Classes should not last longer than 45 minutes to an hour. Ten to 15 minutes several times daily is a good length for at-home practice. End the session at a point when Delilah has successfully obeyed the command or performed the activity being practiced.

✔ Never correct your dog after the fact. Dogs do not share with us our sense of time. They don't connect a scolding with something they did five hours ago, or even five minutes ago. Unless you catch Samson in the act of misbehaving, save the angry words. If you do find him chewing or eliminating where he shouldn't, keep corrections short. Say "No," and either distract him with a toy or take him to the appropriate place to do his business.

When to Begin Training

Your puppy is capable of learning many new things at a rapid pace, so the earlier you start training and socializing your Mastiff, the better off you'll be. The ideal time to begin is when you bring the pup home at 9 to 12 weeks of age. Puppy training techniques and puppy kindergarten classes are discussed in greater detail beginning on page 28. Once your pup has learned the basics, you can reinforce them with practical use at home or go on to more advanced training for Obedience trials.

Training Equipment

For puppy kindergarten, your Mastiff will need nothing more than a flat leather or nylon collar and a leather or nylon leash that is ¾ of an inch (19 mm) wide and 5 to 6 feet (1.5–1.8 m) long. Be sure the collar is sized correctly. You should be able to fit two fingers between the collar and the dog's neck. Check the collar as your puppy grows to see if it needs to be adjusted. The leash should be lightweight but well made. Avoid chain leashes, which can be heavy and noisy.

When you move from puppy kindergarten into a regular obedience class, your trainer may or may not require the use of a training, or choke, collar. If used properly, a choke collar is an effective and harmless training tool, but many trainers today prefer to use as little negative reinforcement as possible. Run, don't walk, from any trainer who advocates choking or hanging the dog with this type of collar!

A training collar may be made of metal or nylon. For a dog the size of a Mastiff, the collar should have medium-size links. Be sure you know how to put it on, or it won't release correctly. Place the collar so that the ring where the lead is attached is on the left side of the neck. To give a correction, simply snap and release the collar, using a quick motion. The intent is to get your dog's attention, not to choke him.

Immediately after every training session, remove the choke collar and replace it with the dog's regular collar. It's very easy for a training collar to get caught on a gate, crate, or even a bit of shrubbery and strangle the dog.

The Polite Mastiff

By the time he is four to six months old, Samson should know the commands *sit, down, stay, sit/stay, down/stay,* and *come.* Instructions for teaching these commands begin on page 34. You can build on this foundation by extending the length of time required for the *stays,* and teaching new commands such as *wait* (to

Build on the basics to teach your puppy tricks such as "shake." Learning new things keeps a dog's mind active.

slow down a dog that is pulling your arm out of its socket), *up* (for getting into the car), and the directions for left and right. As well as knowing these commands, your Mastiff should be house-trained and have some understanding of what's okay to chew and what's not.

Solving Behavior Problems

Aggression

Mastiffs are not mean dogs, but they are huge and imposing, frequently weighing more than their people. If not brought at an early age to a proper understanding of their place in the home, they will quickly learn that their size gives them control. A Mastiff

If you use a chain training collar, remove it if you aren't working with your Mastiff. It can easily get hung up on a fence or other object and choke the dog.

without an owner who provides strong leadership will soon make a play for the leadership role himself: pushing ahead of people, shoving them out of the way, guarding food and toys, and refusing to get off furniture. Other signs of aggression include ignoring commands and mounting people. These behaviors, especially jumping up, are often misinterpreted or ignored until one day Samson, the cute puppy, has turned into a big dog who growls when his dominant behaviors are finally rebuffed. At this point, the help of a qualified behaviorist is usually necessary to straighten out the situation.

To prevent your Mastiff from ever getting to this stage, be alert for problem behaviors—especially if your dog displays three or more of them—when a puppy is young and still malleable. For instance, if Samson pushes ahead of you through doorways, teach him to sit at doorways until you give the signal to come. Instead of retreating when the puppy shoves you or humps your leg, push back, invading his space. Forestall food guarding by frequently taking up a young puppy's food and then returning it. Require Samson to sit before you feed him. Your actions teach the dog that you have the power over food, which is a pack leader prerogative.

Avoid physical force. Use a distraction such as a toy or treat to lure Samson when he is misbehaving—such as refusing to get off the sofa—and then reward him when he comes to you. Make sure he doesn't have the opportunity to get back on the sofa.

Spaying and neutering can reduce aggressive tendencies, as can changing to a diet that is lower in protein. Don't hesitate to ask your veterinarian for advice or for a referral to a veterinary behaviorist or knowledgeable trainer.

Barking

This is not a common problem in Mastiffs, but it can occur if they get bored or lonely. Try to determine why the dog is barking. Rotate toys to prevent boredom, and spend plenty of time with the dog. To deter barking, there are several methods you can try. If you are near Samson, wrap your hand around his muzzle and say *"No bark"* or *"Quiet."* Praise him for being quiet. A shake can works well when you are some distance away. Take an empty soda can, put a few pennies or pebbles in it, and tape the top closed. When the dog barks, throw the can in his direction (don't try to hit him). Ideally, the can will appear to come from nowhere. The noise will startle the dog so he stops barking. Then praise him for being quiet.

For times when you can't be there, a bark-inhibiting collar may work. These collars give off a high-frequency sound when the dog barks. Like a shake can, the sound is intended to distract the dog so that he stops barking. Another type of collar has been developed that emits a mist of citronella scent every time the dog barks. The scent discourages the dog from barking.

Chewing

Mastiffs love to chew, and they'll chew on anything. Attempt to control this habit from the beginning by directing Samson toward appropriate chew toys while he's young. Keep valued items away from those inquiring jaws, and rotate toys frequently so he doesn't get bored. If you see your dog chewing on something he shouldn't, take the item away (without making a fuss) and replace it with an acceptable toy. Then praise the dog for chewing on the toy. Some chewers are deterred by the application of Bitter Apple or hot sauce to plants, furniture, and other items, while others just find that it adds to the flavor.

Inappropriate Elimination

If Samson is six months old or older, has plenty of opportunities to go outside and eliminate, yet still has accidents in the house, your first step should be to take him to the veterinarian to make sure there is nothing physically wrong with him. For instance, spayed females sometimes "leak," a condition that can be controlled with medication. Older dogs may not have the bladder control of their younger years, which isn't something they should be punished for. Put down papers for them to use, or limit them to areas that are easily cleaned.

If the dog is healthy, repeat the house-training process by keeping the dog on a strict feeding and elimination schedule. When you can't be there to supervise, put the dog in his crate or in a confined area with newspapers laid down. Observe the dog carefully for signs that he needs to go out. Some dogs are very subtle in expressing their needs, giving only a brief whine or even just an expectant look when they need to eliminate. Excitement or excessive submission can

Teaching your Mastiff not to jump on people in greeting is essential.

also cause dogs to lose control of their bladders. To help put a stop to this behavior, keep homecomings low-key, and greet young Samson down at his level instead of standing over him. Often, submissive urination is outgrown.

The territorial marking of urine, especially by males, is best controlled by neutering at an early age. Otherwise, use a shake can or water squirter to startle the dog when he starts to lift his leg, and buy lots of stock in companies that make odor-control products.

Jumping Up

Most people incorrectly view jumping up by a dog as an expression of welcome, but it's a dominant behavior that should be discouraged, especially in a giant breed. Teach your puppy that jumping up will be ignored, but sitting is rewarded. If Samson jumps up on you, step back or turn aside so he doesn't make contact. Then tell him to sit. When he complies, give plenty of praise.

Shyness

A common behavior problem in Mastiffs is shyness. Shyness can be congenital, meaning it is an inborn condition, or it can develop during puppyhood from lack of socialization. Mastiffs that are not well socialized can become housebound, preferring to stick close to home and interact only with their own family. This can cause difficulties when your dog needs to leave home to visit the veterinarian, go on a trip, or stay at a boarding kennel.

Socialization is one of the most critical aspects of Mastiff ownership. Take your puppy out and about as often as possible—to the bank, the post office, the dry cleaner, the shopping center. Your Mastiff should meet all kinds of people under many different conditions. Introduce Samson to postal workers and police officers so he becomes accustomed to people in uniform, and arrange a visit to a nursing home or hospital so he can learn about walkers and wheelchairs. Nothing should faze a well-socialized dog.

Should You Let Your Dog on the Furniture?

Mastiffs definitely love their comforts. They are more than willing to share the sofa or bed with you. This can be fun when your Mastiff is a young pup, but you need to take the long view. Will you still enjoy having Samson share your furniture when he weighs 150 pounds (68 kg)? A full-grown Mastiff jumping onto your bed can allow you to experience the sensation of a minor earthquake, and these dogs sprawl. Unless you have a king-size bed, expect your dog to take the lion's—or in this case, Mastiff's—share of it. And a well-used Mastiff sofa will soon bear the indentation of the dog's body.

You can solve the furniture dilemma in one of two ways. The first is to not permit the dog on any furniture at all; once your Mastiff gets a pawhold, all is lost. The second is to teach Samson that he is allowed on the furniture by invitation only or that he is allowed only on certain pieces of furniture.

Consider your dog's temperament when making this decision. A Mastiff that shows any tendencies toward aggression or dominance should not be permitted on furniture at all. It will only give Samson an inflated idea of his importance. Provide comfortable bedding on the floor, and make sure he knows that is his place.

Good Dog, Good Owner

When you bring a dog into your life, the decision affects more than just you and the dog. It affects everyone you and your Mastiff come in contact with, especially your neighbors. You can ensure a happy relationship among all concerned by teaching your dog good manners and practicing responsible pet ownership. This includes training your dog so that it doesn't jump up on people or bark excessively, walking your dog on leash so that it doesn't run wild throughout the neighborhood, providing proper confinement, and picking up waste so that it doesn't attract flies and vermin or foul your neighbors' lawns.

Teaching your Mastiff proper behavior when he's young is perhaps the most important thing you can do, both for your own enjoyment of the dog's companionship as well as for your neighbors' pleasure and peace of mind. If you've ever lived near someone who had an unruly dog, you know how annoying it can be: kids and garbage cans being knocked down, and barking at all hours of the day and night.

To keep the peace and prevent problems from ever starting, be sure your dog is under control—preferably on leash—when other people are around, and avoid situations that might cause your dog to bark unceasingly. These include being frequently left alone for long periods or left without any means of entertainment, such as toys. Fortunately, Mastiffs are not known for being barkers, but their voices are deep and loud: When they do bark, everyone knows it. If your neighbors complain, keep an open, understanding mind, and try to determine the cause of the barking. People will be more patient if they see that you are honestly trying to solve the problem.

UNDERSTANDING DOG SHOWS

Showing a Mastiff in conformation dog shows can be a fun family activity or an outlet for a dog-loving person with a competitive streak. Start by studying the breed standard and learning how to handle a dog in the show ring.

The Dog Show

A dog show is more than just a beauty contest. Dogs are judged on their physical and mental soundness, as well as on how closely they match the breed standard, a written description of the ideal Mastiff.

There are five classes that nonchampion Mastiffs can enter at shows: Puppy, Novice, Bred-by-Exhibitor, American-bred, and Open. Sometimes puppy classes are subdivided into Puppies 6 to 9 months and Puppies 9 to 12 months. In all classes, males compete against males and females against females. Once each class has a winner, they all compete in the Winners class, again separated by sex. A Winners Dog and Winners Bitch are chosen, as well as a Reserve Winners Dog and Reserve Winners Bitch. The reserve winners will take the points if for some reason the win of the Winners Dog or Bitch is disallowed.

Next, Mastiffs that are already champions, plus the Winners Dog and Winners Bitch, compete in the Best of Breed class. The judge also

decides Best of Winners between the Winners Dog and Winners Bitch. If the Winners Dog or Bitch was named Best of Breed, it automatically becomes Best of Winners. Finally, the judge selects Best of Opposite Sex, which is just what it sounds like: the best dog of the sex opposite that of the Best of Breed winner. Then, the Best of Breed winner goes through Group competition and, if it's lucky, Best in Show judging. At some shows, as many as 4,000 dogs may compete in a single day for this coveted award.

To earn a championship, a dog must accumulate 15 points at shows. The number of points earned at each show depends on how many dogs were entered for that breed. Because some breeds are more numerous and are found in a greater number of areas than others, the number of dogs required for points is based on the breed, sex, and show location. Depending on these variables, a dog may earn from one to five points per show. A win that carries three, four, or five points is called a major. The points accumulated toward a championship must

The breed standard details the Mastiff's appearance from head to tail, as well as its gait and temperament.

include wins from three different judges and at least two majors from different judges.

The ease or difficulty of putting a championship on a Mastiff depends a lot on where you live. If you have a nice dog and live in an area that is not heavily populated, earning a championship can be fairly easy. The AKC divides the country into zones, and the number of Mastiffs required to earn points varies from zone to zone. In California, for instance, your dog may have to beat 26 other Mastiffs to earn a major, while a Mastiff in Idaho may have to beat only six other Mastiffs. Some people put championships on their dogs by taking them to show circuits in less-populated zones. The point formula changes each May, depending on how many Mastiffs competed the previous year.

What Is a Breed Standard?

A breed standard is a written description of the physical characteristics of the ideal dog. It is what separates a Mastiff from a Rottweiler from a Great Dane. Each breed has a standard, against which it is judged in the show ring. No dog will meet the standard in all respects; the winner is the dog that most closely meets the standard. Careful breeders know the standard by heart and use it to help make decisions about which Mastiffs to breed to each other to improve the appearance and soundness of the dogs they produce.

A breed standard is not immutable. It may change over the years to permit new colors or to clarify a point that is confusing. Any changes made to the standard are initiated by a breed's parent club and must be voted on and approved by the membership. Then the changes are sent to the AKC's board of directors for their approval. The current breed standard for the Mastiff is available on the web site of the Mastiff Club of America (*www.mastiff.org*) or on the web site of the AKC (*www.akc.org*). Some of the terms used in the standard are explained on page 61.

The Mastiff standard does not contain points for each aspect of the dog's conformation. Rather, faults are noted in each category to help the judge give proper weight to the individual dog's qualities, both positive and negative.

First and foremost, the judge looks for dogs that generally meet the Mastiff standard. They are well balanced, their fronts match their rears, they have nice toplines, and they gait correctly. Dogs that vary too much in type or structure are eliminated from consideration. Then the judge begins to choose the dogs that correspond most closely to the standard.

Official Mastiff Standard

General Appearance—The Mastiff is a large, massive, symmetrical dog with a well-knit frame. The impression is one of grandeur and dignity. Dogs are more massive throughout. Bitches should not be faulted for being somewhat smaller in all dimensions while maintaining a proportionally powerful structure. A good evaluation considers positive qualities of type and soundness with equal weight.

Size, Proportion, Substance—*Size—*Dogs, minimum, 30 inches (76 cm) at the shoulder. Bitches, minimum, 27½ inches (70 cm) at the shoulder. *Fault—*Dogs or bitches below the minimum standard. The farther below standard, the greater the fault.

*Proportion—*Rectangular, the length of the dog from forechest to rump is somewhat longer than the height at the withers. The height of the dog should come from depth of body rather than from length of leg. *Substance—*Massive, heavy boned, with a powerful muscle structure. Great depth and breadth desirable. *Fault—*Lack of substance or slab sided.

Head—In general outline giving a massive appearance when viewed from any angle. Breadth greatly desired.

Eyes set wide apart, medium in size, never too prominent. *Expression* alert but kindly. Color of eyes brown, the darker the better, and showing no haw. Light eyes or a predatory expression is undesirable. *Ears* small in proportion to the skull, V-shaped, rounded at the tips. Leather moderately thin, set widely apart at the highest points on the sides of the skull continuing the outline across the summit. They should lie close to the cheeks when in repose. Ears dark in color, the blacker the better, conforming to the color of the muzzle.

Skull broad and somewhat flattened between the ears, forehead slightly curved, showing marked wrinkles which are particularly distinctive when at attention. Brows (superciliary ridges) moderately raised. Muscles of the temples well developed, those of the cheeks extremely powerful. Arch across the skull a flattened curve with a furrow up the center of the forehead. This extends from between the eyes to halfway up the skull. The *stop* between the eyes well marked but not too abrupt. Muzzle should be half the length of the skull, thus dividing the head into three parts—one for the foreface and two for the skull. In other words, the distance from the tip of the nose to stop is equal to one-half the distance between the stop and the occiput. Circumference of the muzzle (measured midway between the eyes and nose) to that of the head (measured before the ears) is as 3 is to 5.

Muzzle short, broad under the eyes and running nearly equal in width to the end of the nose. Truncated, i.e., blunt and cut off square, thus forming a right angle with the upper line of the face. Of great depth from the point of the nose to the underjaw. Underjaw broad to the end and slightly rounded. Muzzle dark in color, the blacker the better. *Fault*—snipiness of the muzzle.

Nose broad and always dark in color, the blacker the better, with spread flat nostrils (not pointed or turned up) in profile. *Lips* diverging at obtuse angles with the septum and sufficiently pendulous so as to show a modified square profile. *Canine Teeth* healthy and wide apart. Jaws powerful. *Scissors bite* preferred, but a moderately undershot jaw should not be faulted providing the teeth are not visible when the mouth is closed.

Neck, Topline, Body—*Neck* powerful, very muscular, slightly arched, and of medium length.

The neck gradually increases in circumference as it approaches the shoulder. Neck moderately "dry" (not showing an excess of loose skin). *Topline*—In profile the topline should be straight, level, and firm, not swaybacked, roached, or dropping off sharply behind the high point of the rump.

Chest wide, deep, rounded, and well let down between the forelegs, extending at least to the elbow. Forechest should be deep and well defined with the breastbone extending in front of the foremost point of the shoulders. Ribs well rounded. False ribs deep and well set back. *Underline*—There should be a reasonable, but not exaggerated, tuck-up. *Back* muscular, powerful, and straight. When viewed from the rear, there should be a slight rounding over the rump. *Loins* wide and muscular.

Tail set on moderately high and reaching to the hocks or a little below. Wide at the root, tapering to the end, hanging straight in repose, forming a slight curve, but never over the back when the dog is in motion.

Forequarters—*Shoulders* moderately sloping, powerful and muscular, with no tendency to looseness. Degree of front angulation to match correct rear angulation. *Legs* straight, strong and set wide apart, heavy boned. *Elbows* parallel to body. *Pasterns* strong and bent only slightly. *Feet* large, round, and compact with well arched toes. Black nails preferred.

Hindquarters—*Hindquarters* broad, wide and muscular. *Second thighs* well developed, leading to a strong hock joint. *Stifle joint* is moderately angulated matching the front. *Rear legs* are wide apart and parallel when viewed from the rear.

When the portion of the leg below the hock is correctly "set back" and stands perpendicular to the ground, a plumb line

dropped from the rearmost point of the hindquarters will pass in front of the foot. This rules out straight hocks, and since stifle angulation varies with hock angulation, it also rules out insufficiently angulated stifles. *Fault*—Straight stifles.

Coat—Outer coat straight, coarse, and of moderately short length. Undercoat dense,

Standard Definitions

Cow-hocks: Hocks that turn in, with the rear feet toeing out.

Haw: The third eyelid, or nictitating membrane, on the inside corner of the eye.

Hock: In simple terms, the hock is the dog's heel. It is a collection of bones of the hind leg, which form the joint between the second thigh and the metatarsus.

Loin: The area behind the ribs and in front of the pelvic girdle.

Occiput: The back part of the skull.

Pastern: The area of the foreleg between the wrist and toes.

Slab-sided: Flat ribs with too little spring from the spinal column.

Splayfoot: Foot that is flat with spread-out toes.

Stop: The indentation between the eyes where the nasal bones and cranium meet.

short, and close lying. Coat should not be so long as to produce "fringe" on the belly, tail, or hind legs. *Fault*—Long or wavy coat.

Color—Fawn, apricot, or brindle. Brindle should have fawn or apricot as a background color which should be completely covered with very dark stripes. Muzzle, ears, and nose must be dark in color, the blacker the better, with similar color tone around the eye orbits and extending upward between them. A small patch of white on the chest is permitted. *Faults*—Excessive white on the chest or white on any other part of the body. Mask, ears, or nose lacking dark pigment.

Gait—The gait denotes power and strength. The rear legs should have drive, while the forelegs should track smoothly with good reach. In motion, the legs move straight forward; as the dog's speed increases from a walk to a trot, the feet move in toward the center line of the body to maintain balance.

Temperament—A combination of grandeur and good nature, courage and docility. Dignity, rather than gaiety, is the Mastiff's correct demeanor. Judges should not condone shyness or viciousness. Conversely, judges should also beware of putting a premium on showiness.

Approved November 12, 1991
Effective December 31, 1991

Competing with a Mastiff in the conformation ring can be very rewarding. A nice Mastiff who is presented properly is not difficult to finish to a championship. The following tips will help you successfully show this breed.

Tips for Successful Showing

1. Ask your breeder or another person knowledgeable about Mastiffs to evaluate your dog. Of course he looks beautiful to you, but a more clear-eyed evaluation can help you decide if being shown is really right for your dog. A potential show dog must have correct structure,

physical soundness, and a great temperament, being neither shy nor aggressive.

2. Attend handling classes to learn ring etiquette and how to present your dog. Some of the things you might learn include teaching Samson to keep his head up while moving without you having to hold it up with the leash, how to get good expression using a toy or food as bait, and how to stack him. Working to establish leash control and a rapport with the dog are also important.

3. Never get angry with your Mastiff when things don't go as planned. Instead, try to figure out how you can make the

dog's quirks work for you. Setting the lead the same way each time you go in the ring, keeping a special toy handy to hold Samson's attention, and adjusting your stride and direction to that of the dog will help you maintain a smooth and professional appearance. Praise Samson for the things he does well, and accept the things he won't do well.

4. Present a clean, attractive, comfortable dog. Bathe Samson before the show, and give his coat a good brushing. Before you go into the ring, give a final going-over with a soft cloth or chamois. Carry a slobber towel so Samson's mouth is dry for the judge's examination. Be sure he's kept cool before he goes in the ring so he's not panting and uncomfortable when he walks in.

5. Look professional. Not only should your dog be well groomed, you should be dressed appropriately as well. Leave the jeans and T-shirt at home, and wear flat, comfortable shoes for ease of movement in the ring.

6. Prevent boredom. Bring a toy to help ensure that Samson has an alert, interested expression during the judge's exam. His ears should be

Ask an experienced, knowledgeable breeder to help you evaluate your Mastiff.

forward, not back, and his stance should be vigilant, not fidgety or saggy.

7. Make showing fun. Samson should want to be in the ring more than anything else because you've made him feel special and important. The best show dogs enjoy what they're doing. On the other hand, excessive showiness is not correct for the Mastiff's temperament, although some judges tend to ignore that. A dog that barks or wags his tail when offered a piece of bait is generally a crowd pleaser, but a knowledgeable judge will not give him extra points over the correct Mastiff that is sober and does what his handler asks.

8. Present your dog, not yourself. The best handlers are the ones you don't even notice. They know that their job is to make the dog look good and to make the judge think as much of the dog as they do. Remember that the judge is looking at the dog, not at you. Samson should be set squarely on his feet,

with the topline straight and the hocks perpendicular to the ground. He shouldn't be overangulated or too stiff. To see if your Mastiff is set up correctly, draw an imaginary plumb line from the rear of his rump straight down. If the hocks are perpendicular, the line should fall right in front of the toes. The same angulation is correct for the front. A Mastiff with proper angulation is balanced and can move correctly. Mastiffs look best free-stacked. It's nice if you can get them to lean forward slightly while stacked, and the rear legs shouldn't be set too wide.

Praise

Remember that your dog is always a winner, no matter how you place. If you are upbeat and happy, Samson will pick up on your manner. Tell him what a good dog he is, and give him a toy or a treat. Showing will go better if you and the dog always have a good time.

Mastiffs are not the typical canine athletes, but they are well suited to canine sports such as obedience trials, rally obedience, and draft work. Some Mastiffs have even been known to compete in faster-paced dog events such as agility and flyball.

Puppy Play

Mastiff puppies grow quickly and need a lot of rest. Let them play at their own pace, and don't begin forced exercise, such as walks, until they are at least six months old. Before then, your Mastiff puppy's walks should be limited to a distance of about 100 feet (30 m) and back.

Avoid roughhousing as well. Although your young or adolescent Mastiff may look as if he can handle anything, his bones are still forming and are quite vulnerable to injury. Be patient and wait until he is fully grown—two years old—before you begin any activity that requires jumping, such as open obedience or agility.

Activities and Trials

When to Begin Walks

Once your puppy is between four and six months old, the two of you can take very short walks of about a block. At six to seven months of age, you can start working up to several blocks. By the time Samson is a year old, he can be introduced to greater distances. The average adult Mastiff will enjoy a nice, leisurely walk of up to two miles every day. If you like to jog and would like to have canine companionship, you should probably consider another breed. Just as with people, jogging is hard on the Mastiff's joints and can lead to orthopedic problems. When Samson begins to show signs of age, you should probably reduce the length of his walks to about half a mile daily.

Besides walks, there are a number of activities in which you and Samson can participate. He is a working breed, so his power can be put to good use in events such as carting or weight pulling. His good nose makes him suitable for tracking, and his deliberateness stands him in good stead in Obedience trials. And some Mastiffs just wanna have fun, finding enjoyment in the fast-paced sports of agility and flyball. Following is a brief description of some of the sports your Mastiff can enjoy and how to get involved.

Agility

While you wouldn't think that a huge dog such as the Mastiff would do well in an activity whose very name means nimbleness and dexterity, some Mastiffs have taken to it like elephants

You can begin teaching Agility commands such as *go, wait, left, right,* and so on while your dog is a puppy, but again, you should avoid jumps (except for very small ones) until your Mastiff has stopped growing. Be sure your veterinarian checks your dog out first to make sure he is in good condition to begin this sport.

The American Kennel Club sponsors Agility competitions. For more information, contact the AKC, seek out an agility class in your area, or see one of the many books or videos available on the subject.

Draft Work

Besides being guardians of the home, versatile Mastiff-type dogs have been used throughout history to aid in transport of goods and people by pulling carts and wagons. Canine drafting skills aren't widely needed in today's motorized age, but they can still come in handy; a Mastiff who knows how to pull can help out with newspaper routes, unloading groceries, and gardening chores or other yard work. Just for fun, your dog can give rides to neighborhood kids or participate in local parades. Your Mastiff can even take part in draft tests and earn titles.

Before beginning draft work, Samson should know and respond to the commands *stay* and *come.* In class, he'll learn new commands for starting, stopping, and turning. The only equipment you need is a properly fitting padded harness and something for your dog to pull. Some people begin by adapting a child's wagon and then move on to homemade or custom vehicles. For more information, talk to other dog owners. Many dog clubs or breed clubs offer carting classes and events.

to peanuts. Agility is a timed event in which dogs must navigate a directed obstacle course consisting of such items as A-frames, tunnels, weave poles, and hoops. Mastiffs are certainly not the most common breed participating in this sport, but if your dog takes an interest in it, the two of you can have a great time.

It goes without saying that to take up Agility your dog must be sound, as well as willing to try new things. Some beginner obedience classes offer confidence builders such as teaching the puppy to walk on a plastic surface or clear a 6-inch (15 cm) jump. If your Mastiff enjoys these activities, he may be a candidate for Agility. A Mastiff will never win in Agility through speed, but precision is an attainable goal.

Flyball

This fast-paced sport is not one in which Mastiffs commonly compete, but there are individual dogs that love it. If your Mastiff is one of these, flyball is a great way for the two of you to have fun with other dogs and people.

Flyball is a team relay race with each team having four dogs. The dogs must jump four hurdles (set 4 inches [10 cm] below the shoulder height of the shortest dog, with an 8-inch [20 cm] minimum), trigger a spring-loaded box to release a tennis ball, catch the ball, and go back over the hurdles to the starting line, where the next dog is impatiently waiting his turn. The first team to complete the course with no errors wins the heat.

Because it requires jumping, flyball calls for a dog in top orthopedic condition, especially if the team doesn't have a Chihuahua to bring jump heights down. To learn more about flyball or to find a team in your area, contact the North American Flyball Association, listed on page 92.

Obedience Trials

Success in Obedience trials is dependent on precise performance and timing. The thing to remember about Mastiffs is that they are slower and more deliberate than other breeds. You won't get the same upbeat performance from them that you would from Border Collies or Golden Retrievers, but you can still earn titles. Jump heights have been lowered for Mastiffs, so more of them are competing in open classes.

Obedience trials test a dog's ability to perform a specific set of exercises. Obedience titles can be earned at three levels: Novice, for the title Companion Dog; Open, for the title Companion Dog Excellent; and Utility, for the titles Utility Dog and Utility Dog Excellent. For each of these Obedience titles, a dog must earn three "legs," meaning that the dog scores at least 170 out of a possible 200 points, with more than 50 percent on each exercise.

Dogs at the Novice level must heel on leash, stand for examination, heel free (off leash), come when called *(recall)*, and perform a *long sit* (one minute) and a *long down* (three minutes). Open classes consist of the exercises *heel free, drop on recall, retrieve on flat, retrieve over the high jump, broad jump, long sit* (three minutes), and *long down* (five minutes). At the Utility level, the dog must complete a signal exercise (in which he is directed by hand signals with no verbal commands), two scent discrimination tests, a directed retrieve, a directed jump, and stand for group examination.

Rally Obedience

Rally Obedience, also known as Rally O, is best described as a cross between traditional Obedience and Agility. Dog and handler go through 12 to 20 stations, performing a different exercise at each one. Exercises might include such common commands as *sit, stay,* or *down*; various turns; and at advanced levels, jumps. Handlers may be directed to move the dog at a slow, fast, or normal pace. The course is designed by the judge, so each is unique. Each dog-handler team is timed and must achieve a minimum of 70 points to earn a qualifying score. Unlike Obedience trials, handlers may talk to and encourage their dogs as they go through the course. Novice exercises are performed on leash; Advanced and Excellent exercises are off leash with at least one jump. To earn a title at Novice, Advanced, or Excellent levels, dogs must earn three qualifying scores from two different judges.

Good Mastiff Citizenship

If the precision required by Obedience trials doesn't appeal to you and your Mastiff, you may want to go for a Canine Good Citizen award instead. The Canine Good Citizen test rates dogs on their appearance and grooming; willingness to accept the approach of a stranger; ability to sit politely for petting, calm down after play or praise, walk on a loose leash, and walk through a crowd; performance of the *sit, down, stay,* and *come* commands; reactions to other dogs and distractions; and behavior when left alone. This is a less regimented series of exercises than those in Obedience trials, and it is a good test of the skills and behavior every dog should exhibit.

If you need a little help in getting to that point, a trainer can help you prepare for the CGC test, which is usually offered several times a year by local dog clubs. Sneak training in

every chance you get. Praise your puppy every time you see him lying down or sitting, even if you didn't request that action. When your Mastiff earns this title, you can proudly put the initials CGC behind his name, secure in the knowledge that you have a well-behaved dog.

Tracking

The Mastiff has a good nose and can do quite well in Tracking if properly trained. Tracking tests require a dog to follow a trail by scent to earn Tracking Dog (TD), Tracking Dog Excellent (TDX), or Variable Surface Tracking (VST) titles.

TD Test. In the TD test, the track is 440 to 500 yards (402–457 m) long, with a minimum of two right-angle turns, and must be a half hour to two hours old. The person laying the track must be unknown to the dog. At the end of the track, the dog must locate a scent article dropped by the track layer.

TDX Test. The TDX track is 800 to 1,000 yards (731.5–914 m) long, with several turns and two cross tracks. It must be three to five hours old and includes varying terrain such as ditches, streambeds, and tall grass. Dummy scent articles are laid along the trail.

VST Test. Tracking Dog and Tracking Dog Excellent tests usually take place in rural locations, but the VST tests a dog's tracking ability in more developed areas. The VST track length is 600 to 800 yards (549–731.5 m) and must cover a minimum of three types of surfaces, such as asphalt, concrete, grass, gravel, or sand. One-third to one-half of the track must be lacking in vegetation. The track must be three to five hours old with four to eight turns.

A dog that passes all three of the above tests earns the title Champion Tracker (CT).

For more information about the rules and regulations for Tracking tests, contact the AKC (address on page 92).

Search and Rescue

To challenge your dog's abilities beyond the sport level, consider becoming involved in a search and rescue organization. Most search and rescue situations involve looking for lost hikers or wandering children. This can be an exciting and rewarding volunteer activity if your dog is properly trained and you have the orienteering and survival skills required. Members of search and rescue teams—and their dogs—must be in good shape and ready to go at any hour of the day or night.

Therapy Visits

Samson can make a difference in the life of a sick child or nursing home resident simply by his presence. Animal-assisted therapy (AAT) has been proven time and again to lift spirits, lower blood pressure, and improve activity levels and social interaction. The Mastiff's calm, reassuring personality is ideal for therapy work, and the dog is just the right height to make it easy for people confined to beds to pet him.

A good therapy dog is not shy. He enjoys meeting people but doesn't thrust himself on them. He waits to be invited to touch people, so as not to frighten them. Therapy dogs are clean, flea-free, and up to date on their vaccinations. Most organizations involved with AAT have evaluation programs that dogs and people must pass to ensure that they are suited to this rewarding activity. For more information, contact the Delta Society, Therapy Dogs Inc., or Therapy Dogs International, listed on page 92.

Weight Pulling

The Mastiff's powerful physique makes him a natural for this sport, which originated in Gold

Rush-era Alaska to see whose dog could pull the most freight. In modern weight-pulling competitions, dogs are placed in classes according to their weight, and the dog that pulls the most weight for his class wins.

The vehicle being pulled is usually a cart or sled loaded with bags of dog food or other cargo. The dog must pull the vehicle a distance of 16 feet (4.9 m) within an allotted time, usually one minute. In each round, the weight is increased until only one dog remains.

Weight pulling benefits dogs by building muscle, increasing bone mass, and increasing confidence. Even Mastiffs with mild hip dysplasia can take up weight pulling, as long as they are properly conditioned and trained. Light training should begin when your Mastiff is about 18 months old, and he can compete in sanctioned weight pulls at age two. For more information on weight pulling, contact the United Kennel Club, listed on page 92.

Common Mastiff Injuries

Mastiffs are not more prone to injury than any other breed, but their size does make them more likely to suffer certain types of injuries. One of these is cruciate ligament rupture, or torn knee ligaments. Fortunately, orthopedic surgeons can do quite a good job of repairing cruciate ligament ruptures. For less stress on knees and shoulders, don't let Samson jump off furniture. Lift him off or provide steps or a ramp for him to use. To further strengthen and protect knee and shoulder joints, provide plenty of level and uphill exercise, but take downward slopes at a walk.

Like young boys, Mastiff puppies are prone to injuries during that stage of growth when they become gawky and awkward as they adjust to their rapidly changing size. It's common for young puppies to limp from injuries suffered during play or from transient problems such as panosteitis. To keep problems to a minimum, feed a proper diet that doesn't encourage rapid growth, provide puppies with good footing, and avoid letting them play on slick surfaces where they could fall and injure themselves.

A wagging Mastiff tail can seem to have the power of a bullwhip behind it. Tail injuries can occur if a happy Mastiff beats his tail too strongly against a hard surface such as a door or wall. It may sound silly, but make sure Samson has plenty of room to wag, or you could

end up with blood-spattered walls from an injured tail tip, which can take months to heal. Be careful that tails don't get slammed in car doors, either. That injury can end in amputation of part of the tail.

If Samson explores the great outdoors with you, especially in heavily wooded areas, he may pick up foxtails, grasses with spiked tops that can become embedded in a dog's skin. Most foxtails get caught between a dog's toes, but they can also penetrate other areas of the body, including the nose, and cause serious infections. If you can't get the foxtail out, your veterinarian may have to remove it. Antibiotics may be necessary to prevent infection. Ticks are another hazard found in wooded areas and are discussed in the next chapter on pages 87–88.

Like every breed, Mastiffs can be prone to certain genetic problems, and their great size makes them susceptible to orthopedic conditions such as hip dysplasia. It's important to be aware of potential health problems so you can take steps to prevent them. The best way is to buy a puppy whose parents have health certifications for hip, elbows, heart, and eyes.

Like the legendary strongman, Samson, a Mastiff in fine fettle is a grand sight. This massive dog is powerfully built with a muscular frame that is covered with a short, straight, coarse outer coat and a dense undercoat that lies close to the body. An alert, kindly expression shines out of dark brown eyes. Its teeth are healthy and well spaced, with the ideal mouth having a scissors bite. Mastiff puppies are high-spirited, and adult dogs enjoy moderate activity such as daily walks. These dogs tend to be stoic when they're not feeling well, making every effort to keep up a normal appearance and activity level, so you'll need to be observant to pick up on the subtle signs that your Mastiff may be sick.

The Veterinarian

Dogs are creatures of habit, so take note of any unusual change, such as not wanting to eat or go out for a regular walk. Lack of appetite and a low energy level are signs that your Mastiff may need to visit the veterinarian.

Other indications of health problems include unusual weight gain or loss, excessive consumption of water, excessive urination, bad breath, bleeding gums, diarrhea or constipation, or a coat that is dry, dull, or flaky.

Appetite loss, bad breath, or bleeding gums can indicate dental problems. Weight loss can signal parasite infestation, while obesity can be a sign of thyroid deficiency. If Samson begins drinking unusually large amounts of water and subsequently urinating excessively, he should be checked for diabetes or kidney disease.

Poor coat condition may mean that Samson's food isn't providing the nutrients he needs, or that he is affected by internal parasites or a skin problem such as flea allergy dermatitis. Diarrhea is often a sign of intestinal problems or diseases such as parvovirus. By examining your Mastiff on a weekly basis and keeping a diary of his condition, you can get to know what's normal and what's not, bringing changes to your veterinarian's attention before serious problems develop.

Health Concerns

Like other giant breeds, Mastiffs are prone to certain health problems that can be serious or life-threatening. Some are genetic, while others are related to environmental factors such as the type of exercise or amount of food the dog receives. For instance, obesity stresses not only the bones and joints, but also the heart, liver, kidneys, and other organs.

To help prevent certain genetic problems from affecting the breed further, reputable Mastiff breeders perform the following health certifications on all their breeding stock:

- Hip X-rays are taken at or after 2 years of age
- Elbow X-rays are taken at or after 2 years of age
- Orthopedic Foundation for Animals (OFA) heart certification at or after 1 year of age
- Canine Eye Registry Foundation certification of eyes at or after 2 years of age, with annual recertification
- A complete thyroid panel
- University of Pennsylvania cystinuria test at or after 18 months of age.

Really thorough breeders also obtain OFA patella certification, ensuring that the knees are sound. These breeders also seek certification that the dog is free of von Willebrand disease, a bleeding disorder.

Gastric Torsion (Bloat)

One of the most dangerous of the conditions that affect Mastiffs is gastric torsion, or bloat, which is common in large, deep-chested dogs. It occurs when the stomach twists, preventing the release of gas and fluids. What makes gastric torsion so dangerous is that the signs tend to be subtle. Unless bloat is recognized and treatment—usually emergency surgery— initiated immediately, the dog could die. To learn how to recognize bloat, see page 80, Emergency Care.

Samson's chances of suffering bloat can be lessened through careful management of his diet and activity levels. Feed two or more small meals daily rather than one large meal, and limit his exercise and water consumption for two hours before and after he eats.

It's not possible to predict which dogs will develop gastric torsion, but heredity and temperament may be components of the condition. Some lines of Mastiffs seem to be more predisposed to it than others. And one survey showed that Mastiffs with highly sensitive temperaments were more likely to suffer gastric torsion. These dogs become upset easily when their environment is changed, from such simple changes as a new food to more stressful events such as moving to a new home or going to a show.

Hypothyroidism

Mastiffs may develop hypothyroidism—the underproduction of thyroid hormones T3 and T4—a common hormonal disorder in all dogs. Decreased thyroid function usually occurs when the thyroid gland is damaged or destroyed. Causes of damage include immune-mediated inflammation of the thyroid gland or cancer. Hypothyroidism may also be congenital (existing since birth). Suspect hypothyroidism if Samson seems low on energy or mentally lethargic, gains weight, even though he isn't eating more, or develops a dull, dry coat. Other signs of hypothyroidism include dark pigmentation of the skin, hair loss, or scaly skin. In many breeds, hypothyroidism doesn't develop until middle age or the geriatric years, but it can occur at a fairly young age in Mastiffs. Dogs with hypothyroidism can be treated with synthetic thyroid hormone, which is usually given in pill form twice daily. The medication must continue throughout the dog's life.

Cardiomyopathy

Like other large and giant breeds, Mastiffs have a higher incidence of cardiomyopathy, or enlargement of the heart. The cause of cardiomyopathy is unknown, but veterinary researchers suspect it is a genetic problem. Cardiomyopathy is difficult to detect without a cardiac ultrasound exam, but if diagnosed in its early stages, it can be controlled with medication for a time.

Orthopedic Problems

Common inherited conditions in Mastiffs include orthopedic problems such as hip dys-plasia—a deformity of the hip joint—and vari-ous forms of elbow dysplasia. These include ununited anconeal process, occurring when the elbow joint is incorrectly fused to the ulna, resulting in a fracture through the growth plate, which causes lameness; and fragmented coronoid process, in which the elbow joint wears poorly because loose bone fragments or flaps of cartilage irritate and abrade the joint. Another developmental degenerative joint disease that affects Mastiffs is osteochondritis dissecans (OCD), a defect in or degeneration of the cartilage of the shoulders, knees, elbows, or hocks. The severity of hip dysplasia in young puppies can sometimes be influenced by diet and restricted activity, but in severe cases hip surgery or replacement is necessary, especially in large and giant breeds. Surgery is required to repair ununited anconeal process and OCD.

Be aware of the signs of bloat, which can include pacing, restlessness, gagging, shallow breathing, and an appearance of being in pain.

Common nongenetic orthopedic problems include cruciate ligament rupture (torn knee joints) and panosteitis, a sort of "wandering lameness" that affects puppies during their first year. Panosteitis usually goes away on its own; treatment is aimed at reducing pain.

Eye Problems

Among the eye problems that can occur in Mastiffs are progressive retinal atrophy (PRA), cataracts, retinal dysplasia with detachment, glaucoma, entropion, and ectropion. Of these, PRA causes breeders the most concern.

PRA is an inherited degeneration of the retina that causes blindness, and unfortunately it is not treatable. Early, subtle signs of PRA include clinginess, not wanting to leave lighted areas, or unwillingness to walk through dark areas. You can reduce the risk of acquiring a dog that develops PRA by buying only from breeders who have their dogs' eyes examined and cleared by a veterinary ophthalmologist affiliated with the Canine Eye Registration Foundation (CERF). Breeding dogs can and should be certified free of PRA through a DNA test. Buy a puppy only from breeders who can show you proof that both parents have been tested for and proven free of the Mastiff PRA gene mutation.

Cataracts. Most cataracts are also inherited. A cataract is an opacity of the lens, usually appearing white or yellowish. How much the dog's vision is impaired depends on the size and location of cataracts. Thanks to a new technique called phacoemulsification, cataracts can be removed by fragmenting the lens with ultrasonic vibrations and replacing the extracted lens with a clear plastic intraocular lens. This operation is highly successful and returns vision to near normal.

Retinal dysplasia is the abnormal development of the retina and can be inherited (most common) or acquired. In some cases, it's very mild, while in others it leads to blindness. Unfortunately, there is no treatment.

Entropion is a condition in which the eyelids roll inward. It can damage the surface of the cornea and prevent tears from lubricating the cornea.

Ectropion, in which the eyelid rolls outward, exposes the conjunctiva and cornea to irritation and injury.

Both of the above conditions usually require surgical correction.

Epilepsy

Epilepsy, which may be inherited or acquired, is also found in Mastiffs, although it is not common. It is a seizure disorder caused by a temporary dysfunction of the brain. During a seizure, the dog's body may jerk or become rigid. A dog having a seizure may become anxious or excitable, and may vocalize, drool, or lose control of bladder or bowel function. Seizures appear disturbing, but in most cases they are not painful or life-threatening.

There is no screening test for epilepsy, and because it can develop later in life, a Mastiff may have already produced puppies before epilepsy manifests itself. In mild cases, epilepsy can be controlled with medication. If an inherited form of epilepsy is suspected—taking into account such factors as age and lack of evidence of other diseases that might cause seizures—the dog should be spayed or neutered so the condition isn't passed on to another generation.

Cancer

As in all breeds, cancer is becoming more widespread in Mastiffs. Most forms of cancer usually strike older dogs. Take seriously any lumps or bumps you find on your Mastiff and bring them to your veterinarian's attention. Many cancers are treatable if caught in time.

Ear Infections

Because they have floppy ears, Mastiffs can be prone to ear infections. Suspect an ear infection if Samson frequently shakes or scratches at his head and ears, if the ears smell bad or are producing a discharge, or if the ear flap or ear canal appears inflamed. Take him to the veterinarian as soon as you recognize a problem. Keeping the ears clean and dry will help prevent infections.

Skin Conditions

Certain skin conditions can also affect Mastiffs. Allergies are not common, but hot spots and pyoderma can be a problem, and sometimes large calluses form on the elbows and hocks. To help prevent skin problems, institute a good flea-control program, brush the dog regularly, and clean your Mastiff's lips, face, and ears thoroughly after he eats. Food left on the skin can breed bacteria, causing infections. If you notice Samson frequently biting at or licking his skin, especially between the toes, take steps to soothe the area right away, and do your best to keep it dry. Mastiffs do get dermatitis between the toes, which can be very painful, and such self-mutilation can quickly make skin problems worse. Your veterinarian can prescribe medications that will relieve the itch and treat the inflammation.

Skin problems are sometimes linked to low thyroid levels, which can cause changes in serum and subcutaneous fatty acid concentrations that are consistent with a decreased rate of fatty acid metabolism. Fatty acids are necessary for normal

Skin and coat condition are good indicators of a Mastiff's health. Itchy, dry skin, sores, and patches of hair loss are some of the signs of problems.

sive pattern of inheritance. Although cystine stones are not common in Mastiffs, they are more prone to them than other breeds. This type of stone is a rare form that is painful as well as expensive to treat, requiring medication and a special diet. Cystine stones are hard to get rid of, since they form in acidic rather than alkaline urine. Some breeders supplement their Mastiffs with vitamin C, thinking that it helps prevent hip dysplasia, although there is no evidence to support this. Since vitamin C acidifies the urine, a dog that is predisposed to cystine uroliths may start to produce them.

Other conditions that have been seen in Mastiffs include the following:
- Distichiasis (abnormally located eyelashes)
- Macroblepharon (abnormally large eyelid opening)
- Persistent pupillary membranes (blood vessel remnants that remain in the eye)
- Rupture of the anterior cruciate ligament, which helps support the knee
- Hypertrophic osteodystrophy, a nutritionally based developmental disease caused when puppies grow too quickly
- Panosteitis, intermittent lameness caused by rapid growth

healthy skin, so dogs with low thyroid levels can be predisposed to infections by staphylococcus organisms, ubiquitous little devils that take this opportunity to penetrate the skin's normal protective barriers. Thyroid medication and antibiotics can usually clear up the problem.

Cystinuria

Some Mastiffs can suffer from painful cystine stones, caused by the disease cystinuria. This is an inherited metabolic disease. Cystinuria may be caused by a sex-linked or autosomal reces-

Emergency Care

Good habits of observation and knowledge of first aid are vital for dog owners. In an emergency, veterinary help is a must, but sometimes a dog needs immediate care to save his life. Situations that require emergency first aid or quick recognition and response include bleeding, bloat, broken bones, burns, choking, frostbite, heat exhaustion or heatstroke, and shock. By remaining calm and using the following

The First Aid Kit

Ready-made pet first aid kits are available, but you can also assemble one yourself from common household items. Tape or write your veterinarian's phone number in the box where you keep the supplies, as well as the phone number of and directions to the nearest emergency clinic. The following items are part of a well-stocked first aid kit:

- Activated charcoal (available at drugstores) for adsorbing poisons
- Adhesive tape to secure bandages
- Antibacterial ointment or powder for cleaning wounds
- Blunt-tipped scissors to trim hair from wounds and cut bandaging material
- Cotton balls
- Cotton swabs
- Disinfectant solution
- Eyedropper, turkey baster, or syringe to flush wounds
- Gauze pads and rolls to make bandages
- 3 percent hydrogen peroxide to induce vomiting if instructed
- Kaopectate (ask your veterinarian what amount is appropriate to control your dog's diarrhea)
- K-Y jelly or petroleum jelly to lubricate a thermometer
- Needleless syringe for giving liquid medications
- Needle-nose pliers to remove obstructions from the mouth or throat
- Plaster splint for broken limbs
- Povidone iodine to clean wounds
- Rectal thermometer
- Sanitary napkins to help stem blood flow
- Towels
- Tweezers

techniques, you can stabilize Samson until he gets to the veterinarian.

Bleeding

If a wound is gushing bright-red blood, an artery is involved. The blood from a cut vein is dark red and has a more even flow. In either case, apply and maintain direct pressure with a gauze pad or other clean cloth. Secure the pad or have someone hold it in place, and get veterinary help immediately.

Direct pressure is more effective than a tourniquet, and your dog's leg or tail can be damaged by a tourniquet used improperly. Use a tourniquet only if direct pressure fails to control the flow of blood. If a tourniquet is required, use a long piece of fabric such as a necktie, shoelace, or pantyhose. Place it directly above the wound, between the wound and the heart, and tie a half knot. Then put a pencil or stick on top and complete the knot. You should be able to fit a finger beneath the tourniquet when it is in place. Slowly twist the stick to tighten the loop until the bleeding stops. To permit blood flow, release the tourniquet for a few seconds every five to 10 minutes. Then seek veterinary help immediately.

Warning: If used incorrectly, tourniquets can do more harm than good; use one only as a last resort.

If Samson's ear, foot pad, or penis is bleeding, take the injury seriously. Bleeding in these areas can be difficult to control. Apply pressure as described above, and get the dog to a veterinarian.

Less serious bleeding, such as from a scratch or scrape, also requires treatment, although it is not life-threatening. Use povidone-iodine to clean the wound. When the bleeding stops, apply antibiotic ointment. To be sure that there's no damage under the skin, you might ask your veterinarian to give the wound a look.

Bloat

A Mastiff in the early stages of bloat may stand with his head hanging, pace restlessly, or be lethargic. Mastiffs with bloat often seem to want to be alone. The dog may gag or make unsuccessful attempts to vomit, producing only excess saliva. Shallow breathing and a dull, vacant, or pained expression are other early indicators. The abdomen may appear distended, sounding hollow when thumped. In later stages, the dog will retch or salivate, his pulse will weaken, his gums will grow pale, and he will be unable to stand. If you suspect bloat, do not wait to take the dog to the veterinarian, even if it's the middle of the night. The earlier bloat is discovered, the more likely your dog is to survive. If you're afraid you won't recognize whether the dog's abdomen is expanding, use a tape measure at the level of the last rib to find the dog's normal abdominal size. Jot the information down and put it with your first aid kit. Use the measurement as a baseline any time you suspect bloat.

Broken Bones

Broken bones can be caused by falls, run-ins with cars, or gunshot wounds. If Samson breaks a bone, try to keep him as still as possible. A fracture can become more serious if the broken limb is moved too much. Wrap him in a blanket to help prevent shock, be sure he is cushioned during the car ride, and get to the veterinary hospital at once.

Shock

Shock is a common result of serious injury. In this potentially fatal condition, the body is unable to maintain adequate blood pressure. Vital organs such as the brain, heart, and lungs don't get enough oxygen-rich blood and thus can't function properly. If Samson has been hit by a car or suffered some other injury, he may go into shock. Blood loss, poisoning, or severe fluid loss from vomiting or diarrhea can also cause him to go into shock. A dog that is in shock has a weak, rapid pulse, dry gums and pale or gray lips, shallow, rapid breathing, a low body temperature, and is weak or lethargic. Control any bleeding, keep the dog still and warm, and seek immediate veterinary help.

Spinal Injuries

Spinal injuries can occur when a dog falls from a great height or is hit by a car. Assume a spinal injury if Samson is paralyzed, his legs are rigid, stiff, or limp, or his head is thrust backward. If this is the case, move your dog as little and as carefully as possible. Improvise a stretcher using a board large enough to support the dog's back. Tape or otherwise secure the dog to the board so he won't roll off or move around. If a board is not available, you can use a blanket pulled taut. If possible, slide Samson onto the stretcher instead of lifting him. Treat him for shock as needed, and try to keep him as still as possible during the ride to the veterinary hospital. Your dog will no doubt be frightened and in pain, so talk to him soothingly.

Trauma

If Samson is hit by a car or suffers some other trauma and his lower jaw is hanging open and he is drooling, his jaw may be fractured. Tie a bandage or scarf underneath his chin, fastening it behind the ears, and get him to a veterinarian.

A dizzy or unconscious dog, or one with a bloody nose, may have a skull fracture. Gently control any bleeding, and get veterinary help immediately.

Burns

A burn to Samson's paws or fur should be bathed with cool water or treated with a cool compress. Use cool water only, never ice, butter, or ointment of any kind. Ice can damage the skin, and butter and ointments hold the heat in. If a large area of the body is burned, cover it with a thick layer of gauze or cloth (cotton balls or cotton batting will stick to the damaged skin), keep the dog warm to prevent shock, and get him to a veterinarian right away.

Substances such as battery acid or some toilet bowl cleaners can cause chemical burns. This type of burn can be treated in the same manner as other burns, but be sure to protect your hands by wearing rubber gloves. Seek immediate veterinary treatment.

Puppies and adolescent dogs are likely to chew on electrical cords, leading to the possibility of electrical burns on the corners of the mouth or on the tongue and palate. In the case of electrical shock, Samson may convulse or lose consciousness, his respiration may slow,

Mastiffs love to be with people. Changes in normal behavior, such as hiding, may signal that your dog doesn't feel well.

and severe shock may cause the heart to stop beating. If you find Samson in this condition, don't touch him until you switch off the electrical source, then get him to a veterinarian right away. If you know how to perform CPR on dogs, do not initiate it unless you are sure the heart has stopped; otherwise, you could cause more damage.

Choking

Putting things in his mouth is a large part of a dog's investigative process, and young Mastiffs love to chew. Any time you see Samson cough-

Avoid letting your Mastiff become overheated. Limit exercise on hot days, and be sure he has access to plenty of fresh water and a cool area where he can rest.

ing, gagging, or pawing at his mouth, check for an obstruction. (An especially common obstruction is a piece of bone caught between the upper molars or stuck crosswise in the throat.) Open the mouth by pressing your thumb and forefingers into the upper cheeks. Gently try to remove the obstruction with your fingers or a pair of needle-nose pliers. If you can't remove the object, perform the Heimlich maneuver by standing behind the dog, encircling its abdomen with your arms just beneath or behind the rib cage, and compressing the chest. Repeat until the object is coughed up. If you can't remove it, get the dog to a veterinarian immediately.

Frostbite

Dogs in less than peak condition—those that are very young, very old, or sick—are most prone to frostbite, especially if they are short-haired like the Mastiff. Frostbite is a painful condition that results from prolonged exposure to very cold temperatures. The areas likely to be affected are the footpads, tail, and ear tips. Frostbite is indicated by skin that becomes pale, then reddens and becomes hot and painful to the touch; swelling; and peeling of external skin layers. Keep the frostbitten dog warm, but thaw frostbitten areas slowly. Massaging the skin or applying hot compresses can worsen the damage; instead, apply warm, moist towels and change them frequently. When the skin regains its normal color, stop warming it. Wrap Samson in a blanket to help prevent shock, and get him to a veterinarian right away.

Heat Exhaustion and Heatstroke

Dogs have few sweat glands that perform a cooling function, so they control their body temperature by panting. As the dog pants, body heat evaporates from the mouth. If the dog is unable to disperse heat quickly enough, his body temperature can rise to a dangerous level. This is especially true for short-nosed dogs and large or giant breeds. Mastiffs can easily become overheated if left in a car on a warm day, even if the windows are cracked, or in other situations where the environmental temperature is high.

Heat exhaustion is associated with excessive exercise on hot days, but the dog's temperature doesn't necessarily rise to dangerous levels. A dog with heat exhaustion may collapse, vomit, or have muscle cramps.

Heatstroke can develop in only a few minutes, the body temperature rising to 108°F (42.2°C) or higher. If Samson has heatstroke, he can die if he is not immediately cooled and taken to a veterinarian. Wet his body with cool, not cold, water, and get him to a veterinarian.

Puncture Wounds

This type of wound can be caused by a bite or by a sharp object entering the dog's paw or other area of the body. If not treated properly, a puncture wound can become infected or abscessed. Signs of infection include swelling, redness, warmth, and pain. Sometimes pus collects in the wound, forming an abscess.

Cleanse a bite or puncture wound by flushing the area with a mild disinfectant such as 0.0001 percent povidone-iodine or 0.05 percent chlorhexidine. It's a good idea to take Samson to the veterinarian within 24 hours for a course of antibiotics, especially with bite wounds, which become infected easily. Your veterinarian probably won't stitch up a bite wound because the area will need to drain if it becomes infected.

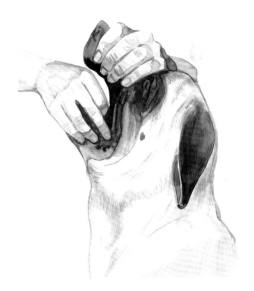

To give a pill successfully, place it in the back of the dog's mouth. Then hold the mouth closed and gently stroke the throat until the pill goes down.

Giving Medication

At some point in his life, it's likely that Samson will need some form of medical care at home. Knowing how to give a pill, administer liquid medications, or place eye- and eardrops is an important complement to regular veterinary care, ensuring that the home care he receives will support the treatment prescribed by the veterinarian. By learning how to give a pill or take your dog's temperature, you will be less likely to panic if he becomes ill, and the dog will be more amenable to receiving the medication and treatment he needs.

Fortunately, Mastiffs are pretty good about taking their medicine, but the more skilled you are, the easier it will be. Remain calm and patient, and the whole thing will be less stressful for both of you. A treat or praise afterward may help your dog view medicine time as more pleasant.

Giving Pills

Some lucky pet owners have dogs that will eat pills mixed with their food. If this is not the case in your household, or if Samson has lost his appetite, the following techniques will help you get pills into him.

With the pill in your right hand, gently open the dog's jaws with your left first and middle fingers. Place the pill far back on the tongue, then close the mouth and hold it closed while stroking the throat. Another technique that works well is to hold the dog's head in your left hand. Tip the head back until the dog is looking straight up. Holding the pill between the thumb and forefinger of your right hand, open the mouth with the middle finger of your right hand. Drop the pill into the back of the mouth and push it over the tongue with the index finger of your right hand. Close the mouth and blow into your dog's nose to make him lick, thus inducing swallowing. If you are left-handed, just reverse these directions. Some pills have an unpleasant flavor if they are broken, so try to give a whole pill whenever possible.

If the above methods don't work, disguise the pill by wrapping it in a tempting treat such as cream cheese, liver sausage, or peanut butter. Unless Samson is extremely picky, he won't even realize the pill is there. Be sure to check with your veterinarian to make sure this method won't affect the pill's efficacy.

It's important to have an effective pill-giving technique so the dog receives the entire amount prescribed at the appropriate times each day. Even if Samson appears to be well, continue giving the medication until it is all finished. Your veterinarian prescribed that amount for a reason, so don't engage in second-guessing.

Liquids

Fill a medicine dropper or syringe with the appropriate amount of medication. Restrain your Mastiff as described above. Tilting the head upward, open the mouth and aim the dropper at the cheek pouch. Holding the mouth closed around the dropper, squeeze out the medication. The automatic swallowing reflex will kick in as the liquid reaches the back of the mouth. Another good way to induce swallowing is by blowing into Samson's nose to make him lick.

Eardrops

Tilt the head slightly to the opposite side. Administer the required amount of medication; then gently hold the ear flap closed and massage the cartilage at the base of the ear. The massaging action gets the medication into the ear, ensuring that less of it is lost if Samson

Ear infections can be difficult to control. Complete the entire course of treatment, even if it looks as if the infection has cleared up.

shakes his head. This massage will feel good to Samson unless his ears are unusually painful.

Eyedrops

Hold Samson's head firmly so he doesn't shake it, causing you to poke him in the eye. With the eyedrop applicator in your right hand (reverse this if you are left-handed), tilt the head upward and place the drops in the inner corner of the eye, directly on the eyeball. Avoid touching the eye with the tip of the applicator. Close and open the eyelids to ensure that the medication is distributed evenly.

Ointments

Ointments generally are applied to a dog's eyes or ears. To medicate eyes, hold Samson's head firmly. Gently pull down on the lower lid, exposing the inner eyelid. Apply the ointment to the inside lower lid, avoiding direct application to the eyeball. You may also pull back the upper lid and place the ointment on the white of the eye. Then close the dog's eyelids to distribute the medication. To apply ointments to ears, follow the directions above for eardrops.

Flea Control

Although not strictly medications, flea-control products contain chemicals that can affect your dog's health. Use these products with care, and follow the directions on the label. Just as with medications, age can be a factor. Note whether the product is safe for puppies and old dogs. If you are treating both your home and your dog for fleas, avoid mixing types of products except under veterinary supervision, as some chemicals can have a toxic effect when mixed. Early signs of chemical poisoning include excessive salivation and nervous tremors, fol-

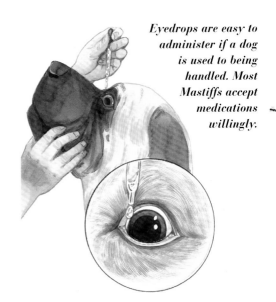

Eyedrops are easy to administer if a dog is used to being handled. Most Mastiffs accept medications willingly.

lowed by collapse, convulsions, and coma. Manufacturers of flea-control products have worked hard to develop safe, effective methods of control, and to a large extent they have succeeded. Several new products are available that are toxic only to fleas, not to dogs. Ask your veterinarian to advise you about which of these flea-fighting methods is best for your situation. For more on flea control, see page 86.

Use of Human Medications

There are some instances in which your veterinarian may recommend giving a medication common in human use, such as Dramamine for carsickness, hydrogen peroxide to induce vomiting, and Kaopectate for diarrhea. Give these drugs to your dog only under veterinary supervision, and ask your veterinarian what dosage is correct for your dog. Never give medications of any type without first asking your veterinarian's advice.

Your Dog's Temperature

You may need to take your dog's temperature if you suspect heatstroke or infection. Normally, a dog's temperature ranges from 100° to 102.5°F (37.8–39°C), with the danger level at 106°F (41.1°C) or higher. To take your dog's temperature, lubricate a rectal thermometer with petroleum jelly, K-Y jelly, or vegetable oil, and gently insert the thermometer into the rectum. For greater safety, use a digital instead of a glass thermometer. Sometimes it's helpful to have someone else hold the dog while you insert the thermometer. Remove the thermometer after one minute. Call your veterinarian if the dog's temperature is nearing or above the danger level, or if the temperature increases throughout the day or on consecutive days.

External Parasites

Fleas, ticks, and mites are all external parasites that can affect your dog. A parasite is an organism that makes its living off other life forms. Fleas and ticks, for instance, get their sustenance by sucking the blood of their victims. Parasites can spread disease and even play a role in the transmission of other parasites, such as tapeworms, to your dog. Keeping your dog free of parasites is an important part of his overall good health.

Fleas

Fleas are a dog's most common and annoying external parasite. Unless you live in a hot, dry climate or a very cold climate, your dog is likely to suffer from the constant itching caused by the bites of these pests. Some dogs are so sensitive to flea saliva—the substance that causes the itch—that a single bite can send them into a frenzy of scratching and biting at the sensitive area. These dogs suffer from a condition called flea allergy dermatitis, which manifests itself in severe itching, crusty sores on the dog's body, and thickening of the skin. Bacterial skin infections are often a secondary response.

Fortunately, Mastiffs have short coats, so it's easier to find fleas on them than it is on long-haired breeds. To determine if Samson is infested with fleas, run a fine-toothed flea comb through his coat. Even if you find only

Lots of handling when your Mastiff is young will make it easier to administer medication when necessary.

one or two fleas, it's evidence that there are probably a lot more biding their time in your house. Another way to scout out fleas is to brush your dog while he's standing over a white cloth or piece of paper. If small black flecks fall onto the white area, moisten them to see if they turn red. When this happens, what you've discovered is flea dirt, or the blood excreted by the flea after it has fed on your dog.

There are many good flea-control products on the market. The newest ones are harmful only to fleas, not to dogs, putting fleas out of commission by attacking their nervous systems or reproductive abilities. Ask your veterinarian to help you determine the best product for your Mastiff, based on the climate in your area and your dog's lifestyle. A dog that spends a lot of time outdoors may need a different regimen than one that is primarily a house or show dog.

Ticks

Ticks belong to the arachnid family. They have tear-shaped bodies with eight legs and generally are brown or black in color. An adult female tick is about the size of a sesame seed. While not as common as fleas, ticks can pose more serious problems. Using their sharp mouthpieces, ticks attach themselves to a dog's skin, most commonly around the head, neck, ears, or feet. A large number of ticks feeding on a single dog can cause severe anemia or tick paralysis, and ticks transmit Lyme disease, Rocky Mountain spotted fever, ehrlichiosis, tularemia, and babesiosis, all of which also can be transmitted to humans, sometimes with severe consequences. There are five main species of ticks in North America: the deer tick, the western black-legged tick, the Lone Star tick, the Rocky Mountain wood tick, and the American dog tick. The deer tick and the western black-legged tick are known to transmit Lyme disease, babesiosis, and ehrlichiosis. Rocky Mountain wood ticks and American dog ticks carry Rocky Mountain spotted fever and tularemia, while the Lone Star tick is known for ehrlichiosis and tularemia. None of these conditions are pleasant for people or dogs and can be debilitating or even deadly, so take every precaution against them.

Ticks are out in full force in spring and summer. Any time Samson has been outdoors, especially in a heavily wooded area, you should examine him for ticks. Wearing gloves, carefully part the fur and look down close to the skin. Unless they're already bloated with blood, ticks can be easy to miss, especially on dogs with dark coats.

To remove a tick, grasp at its head with tweezers, forceps, or one of the many commercially available tick-removal devices. Pull the tick out slowly yet firmly so you don't leave any part of it behind. Spraying the tick with a flea-and-tick insecticide before removal can help loosen the tick's grasp. Never try to burn the tick off; you'll succeed only in injuring your dog. Other methods that should be avoided are covering the tick with nail polish, petroleum jelly, kerosene, or gasoline. Be sure you don't touch or crush the tick with your bare hands. The spirochete that causes Lyme disease can enter through your skin. Once it's removed, kill the tick by dropping it in alcohol. If the head of the tick remains in your dog's body, don't worry about it. Simply clip the hair around the area and bathe the skin lesion with hydrogen peroxide, alcohol, or soap and water for three or four days.

Many sprays, shampoos, dips, and spot-ons are available that will help kill or repel ticks. Your veterinarian can advise you about what is appropriate for your area and situation. If your veterinarian thinks the risk of infection warrants it, your Mastiff can be vaccinated for Lyme disease. Usually, the vaccine is recommended only if there is a high incidence of Lyme disease in the area or if the dog's lifestyle puts it at risk.

Mites

Like ticks, mites are also arachnids, microscopic in size. Four species of mites can infest dogs: *Demodex canis,* which causes canine demodicosis, sometimes known as demodectic mange; *Sarcoptes scabei* var. *canis,* which causes canine scabies, also known as sarcoptic mange; *Cheyletiella,* which causes a mild, itchy skin disease; and *Otodectes cynotis,* or ear mites.

Internal Parasites

The most common internal parasites that affect dogs are roundworms, hookworms, whipworms, tapeworms, and heartworms. Internal parasites are a serious problem because, among other things, they can consume nutrients a dog needs or prevent the dog's body from properly absorbing those nutrients, destroy red blood cells, causing anemia, damage or kill tissues and cells as they move through the body, and transmit disease. If the infection is severe, some internal parasites, such as heartworms, can even kill a dog.

Roundworms

Most dogs have been infected with roundworms *(Toxocara canis)* at one time or another in their lives, most likely at birth. Even if the mother was dewormed during pregnancy, she can still transmit roundworms through her milk. In adult dogs roundworms rarely cause serious problems, but puppies can be severely affected and may even die from a heavy load of roundworms.

A puppy with a bellyful of worms is thin and scrawny, except for a potbelly, and his coat is rough and dull. Vomiting and diarrhea are common signs of roundworm infection, and the puppy may have a cough or even develop pneumonia. Avoid buying a Mastiff puppy with these signs. If it's too late and you've already acquired such a pup, take him to your veterinarian for treatment with a dewormer.

Roundworm transmission to people is rare, but young children can acquire them by touching egg-laden feces or playing in dirt or grassy areas where roundworm eggs have been deposited, and then putting their hands in their mouths. Roundworm infection can be prevented by keeping the yard clean of feces, which should be picked up daily. Adult dogs should have an annual fecal exam so they can be treated for any worms that may be present.

Hookworms

Mastiffs that live in the southern United States or any other area with a warm, humid climate are more likely to fall victim to hookworms than are Mastiffs in dry climates. Hookworms can penetrate the skin, usually through the feet, or they can be transmitted to pups through their mother's milk. Once they migrate through the body to the small intestine, hookworms latch onto the intestinal wall and suck blood from it, causing anemia in severe cases. Diarrhea, weakness, and weight loss are other signs of hookworm infection. To confirm an invasion of hookworms, your veterinarian will need to examine a stool sample for hookworm eggs. Medication can be given to kill the worms,

but unless feces are picked up often, infection will recur quickly.

Whipworms

Like hookworms, whipworms *(Trichuris vulpis)* feed on blood, but they live in the large intestine. They are transmitted when the dog eats something that has been in contact with contaminated soil or infective larvae. Mild infections usually don't cause a problem, but anemia, diarrhea, and weight loss can occur when too many whipworms inhabit the dog. Because their eggs are passed only occasionally, whipworms can be difficult to diagnose, and it may take several fecal exams before their presence is confirmed. As with other internal parasites, there are drugs that will kill the worms, but only a regular yard clean-up program will prevent reinfection.

Tapeworms

Tapeworms look like long, flat ribbons. They have hooks or suckers on their heads, which they use to attach themselves to their host. Fleas play a role in the tapeworm life cycle by eating tapeworm eggs. The immature tapeworms remain in the flea's intestine. When a dog eats that flea, the tapeworm continues its life cycle inside the dog.

The most common type of tapeworm found in dogs is called *Dipylidium caninum*, which is spread by fleas. Tapeworm is often indicated by white, ricelike worm segments crawling on your dog's rear end or in its bedding or stool. Your veterinarian can prescribe medication to get rid of the tapeworms, and good flea-control measures will help keep them away.

Other tapeworms that affect dogs are less common. They include *Taenia pisiformis*, hosted mainly by rabbits, and *Echinococcus*

granulosus, hosted by sheep. The best way to prevent them is to not let your dog eat dead animals. Like *Dipylidium caninum,* these types of tapeworms are diagnosed through stool samples and can be treated with medication prescribed by your veterinarian.

Heartworms

It used to be that only Mastiffs living in the warm, humid climate of the southern United States needed to worry about heartworm infection, but these killers have now spread throughout the country. Transmitted by the bite of a mosquito, heartworm larvae develop in subcutaneous tissues and then enter the bloodstream, which carries them to their final destination—the pulmonary arteries and the right side of the dog's heart. There, they reach maturity, sometimes growing to a length of 12 inches (30 cm), and produce young called microfilariae. When a mosquito bites the dog, it ingests the microfilariae, which go through a developmental stage in the mosquito's body and are then deposited through the mosquito bite into a dog's bloodstream, beginning the life cycle all over again.

When adult heartworms become numerous enough, they can cause such signs as lack of energy, weight loss, coughing after exertion, and eventually congestive heart failure. Diagnosis requires a blood test and sometimes X rays. Treatment usually takes place over a six-week period and requires administration of drugs that are dangerous not only to the heartworms but also to the dog. Doses of a drug to kill the adult heartworms are given intravenously over a two-day period. (In severe cases, the heartworms must be removed surgically.) Several days later, the heartworms begin dying and are absorbed by the body. During this time, which lasts for several weeks, Samson must exert himself as little as possible to avoid the risk of a mass of worms entering the lungs and compromising blood flow there. Medication to kill immature heartworms is given four to six weeks after the first treatment.

Heartworm infection is easily prevented with medications that can be given either daily or monthly, depending on your preference. Some heartworm medications also kill roundworms and hookworms.

Your Aging Mastiff

The Mastiff lifespan generally ranges from six to ten years, with a few hardy dogs living to their early or mid-teens. Mastiffs that are most likely to have an extended lifespan are those whose weight has been kept under control, keeping them free from orthopedic problems and heart disease. As with most dogs, unneutered males tend to have the shortest lifespan; spayed females the longest.

As Samson's years increase, he will become less active but still capable of enjoying life, albeit as an observer rather than a participant. To ensure him a long, healthy life, start when he is a puppy by providing a complete, balanced diet and regular veterinary care. When he starts getting on in years, at about age five, take him to the veterinarian for a geriatric exam. The examination and tests your veterinarian performs will help establish a baseline of good health, against which your dog can be judged as he grows older. Such an exam can also catch problems in their early stages, while they are still treatable. In addition, you can take some simple steps to make life easier for your aging Mastiff.

1. Be sure he has a comfortable bed in a warm place. His bones are a little achier now, so anything you can do to ease his joints will be appreciated.
2. Take him out to eliminate more often. Very young puppies and old dogs don't have the holding capacity of dogs in their prime. Save your carpet and Samson's dignity by ensuring that he has plenty of opportunities to eliminate outdoors. If extra trips during the day aren't possible due to your work schedule, put down papers so he has an acceptable place to go.
3. Keep up the exercise. Samson will still enjoy a walk, with plenty of opportunities to sniff the scent messages left by canine pals.
4. Schedule an annual dental cleaning. Periodontal disease can make your dog's teeth ache, and he will be less inclined to eat if his mouth hurts. Regular brushing, plus a thorough veterinary cleaning, will keep teeth and gums in good shape.

The End of a Life

As everything must, even a beloved Mastiff's life comes to an end. When Samson is very old and no longer enjoying life—refusing to eat and incapable of going for the walks that once meant so much—it is time to talk to your veterinarian about euthanasia. The last gift you can give your dog is a peaceful, pain-free death. A caring veterinarian will permit you to stay with your dog while the injection is given.

Afterward, feel no shame in grieving. The love of a dog is precious and not to be trivialized. It may comfort you to make a donation in Samson's memory to canine health research or to an animal welfare organization. Then it will be time to start thinking about bringing another Mastiff into your life.

Organizations

Mastiff Club of America
www.mastiff.org

American Kennel Club
  Registration and Information
5580 Centerview Drive, Suite 200
Raleigh, NC 27606-3390
(919) 233-9767
www.akc.org

ASPCA Animal Poison Control Center
(888) 426-4435
A $60 consultation fee may be charged
to your credit card.

Delta Society
875 124th Avenue, NE #101
Bellevue, WA 98005
(425) 679-5500
www.deltasociety.org

North American Flyball Association
1400 W. Devon Avenue, #512
Chicago, IL 60660
(800) 318-6312
www.flyball.org

Therapy Dogs, Inc.
P.O. Box 20227
Cheyenne WY 82003
(877) 843-7364
www.therapydogs.com

Therapy Dogs International
88 Bartley Road
Flanders, NJ 07836
(973) 252-9800
www.tdi-dog.org

United Kennel Club
100 East Kilgore Road
Kalamazoo, MI 49001-5598
(269) 343-9020
www.ukcdogs.com

Rescue Groups

Mastiff Club of America
www.mastiff.org/rescue/rescue_index.htm

Books

  Some of these books may be out of print
but can be found through book search firms, at
dog shows, or through some Mastiff web sites.

Dee Dee Andersson, *The Mastiff: Aristocratic
  Guardian.* Wilsonville, OR: Doral Publishing,
  1999.
Elizabeth J. Baxter and Patricia B. Hoffman,
  The History and Management of the Mastiff.
  Wenatchee, WA: Dogwise Publishing, 2004.
Christina De Lima-Netto, *Mastiff: A Compre-
  hensive Guide to Owning and Caring for
  Your Dog.* Allenhurst, NJ: Kennel Club Books,
  2003.
Douglas B. Oliff, *The Mastiff and Bullmastiff
  Handbook.* New York, NY: Howell Book
  House, 1988.

Publications

MCOA Journal. This magazine is $21 per year
for two issues. Subscription information is
available online at *http://www.mastiff.org/
journal/journal_index.htm*

The Mastiff Reporter. Available online at
http://devinefarm.net/reporter/

Video

Call or write to order the AKC Mastiff DVD:

The American Kennel Club
Attention: Video Fulfillment
5580 Centerview Drive #200
Raleigh, NC 27606
(919) 233-9780

The price is $27.95.

For advice on training, check out *See Jane Train Spot*, a one-hour video that features Mastiffs. To order, contact:

See Jane Videos
6991 E. Eaton-Albany Pike
Eaton, IN 47338
JawgDogg@cs.com

The price is $28.

Web Sites and Mailing Lists

A number of mailing lists and web sites are devoted to Mastiffs. For a comprehensive guide of mailing lists, go to *http://devinefarm.net/maillist.htm*

Many Mastiff breeders have home pages featuring their dogs. Do a search for Mastiffs, and you're sure to come up with many of them, as well as pages on Mastiffs in other countries.

The Author

Kim Campbell Thornton, a longtime member of the Dog Writers Association of America (DWAA), has written more than 20 books about dogs, including *Bloodhounds*, a Barron's Complete Pet Owner's Manual. She is the winner of eight DWAA Maxwell Awards, including one for her MSNBC.com column *Creature Comforts*, plus three DWAA Special Awards. Kim and her husband, Jerry, founded the Darcy Fund to raise money for research into the causes of and treatment for chronic valvular disease in Cavalier King Charles Spaniels. They share their home with three Cavaliers and one African ringneck parakeet.

I N D E X

Cover Photos

Front cover: Shutterstock; inside front cover: Pets by Paulette; inside back cover: Jean Fogle; back cover: Shutterstock.

Photo Credits

Jean Fogle: page 16; Isabelle Francais: pages 2–3, 4, 5, 7, 9, 12, 13, 14, 17, 18, 21, 22, 24, 25, 26, 28, 29, 32, 36, 37, 38, 40, 41, 43, 44, 45, 46, 47, 48, 49, 51, 52, 54, 56, 57, 58, 59, 61, 64, 65, 66, 68, 69, 70, 71, 72, 73, 75, 76, 77, 78, 81, 82, 86, 89, 90, and 93; Pets by Paulette: page 20; Kim Campbell Thornton: page 11; Toni Tucker: page 31.

Important Note

This pet owner's guide tells the reader how to buy and care for a Mastiff. The author and the publisher consider it important to point out that the advice given in the book is meant primarily for normally developed puppies from a reputable breeder; that is, dogs of excellent physical health and good temperament.

Anyone who adopts a fully grown Mastiff should be aware that the animal has already formed basic impressions of human beings. The new owner should watch the dog carefully, including his behavior toward humans, and should meet the previous owner. If the dog comes from a shelter, it may be possible to get some information on his background and peculiarities.

There are dogs that, for whatever reason, behave in an unnatural manner or may even bite. Under no circumstances should a known "biter" or an otherwise ill-tempered dog be adopted or purchased as a pet or show prospect.

Caution is further advised in the association of children with dogs, in meeting with other dogs, and in exercising the Mastiff without a leash.

Even well-behaved and carefully supervised dogs sometimes do damage to someone else's property or cause accidents. It is therefore in the owner's interest to be adequately insured against such eventualities, and we strongly urge all dog owners to purchase a liability policy that covers their dog.

Acknowledgments

The author's sincere thanks go to all the Mastiff people who so generously shared their time and knowledge of the breed: Mike Gensburger, Jodie Green, Tom and Cheryl Heard, Debbie Jones, Jan McNamara, Naydene Mitchell, and Robin Smith, DVM.

A Note on Pronouns

Many dog lovers feel that the pronoun "it" is not appropriate when referring to a beloved pet. For this reason, Mastiffs are referred to as "Samson" or "he" throughout this book unless the topic specifically relates to female dogs. No gender bias is intended by this writing style.

All inquiries should be addressed to:
Barron's Educational Series, Inc.
250 Wireless Boulevard
Hauppauge, NY 11788
www.barronseduc.com

Library of Congress Control No. 2008937898

ISBN-13: 978-0-7641-4143-0
ISBN-10: 0-7641-4143-0

Printed in China

9 8 7 6 5 4 3 2 1